THE NEW
BEADWORK

THE NEW
BEADWORK

Kathlyn Moss and Alice Scherer
with
Photography by Tommy Olof Elder

Harry N. Abrams, Inc., Publishers

For
Dennis Moss, Adriane Moss,
and
Howard Newcomb

FRONTISPIECE:
LINDSAY OBERMEYER

Garden of the Soul. 1988. See page 69.

PROJECT DIRECTOR: Margaret L. Kaplan
EDITOR: Eve Sinaiko
DESIGNER: Darilyn Lowe Carnes

Library of Congress Cataloging-in-Publication Data

Moss, Kathlyn, 1944–
    The new beadwork / Kathlyn Moss and Alice Scherer ; with
original photography by Tommy Olof Elder.
        p.   cm.
    Includes bibliographical references (p.   ) and index.
    ISBN 0–8109–3670–4
    1. Beadwork. I. Scherer, Alice, 1953–   II. Title.
TT860.M67   1992
745.58′2—dc20

                                                    92-6747
                                                        CIP

Printed and bound in Hong Kong

Contents

JEANNINE GORESKI

Red Bowl. 1988. See page 41.

Foreword

I love beadwork. For me it hits a primal nerve, combining color, texture, and sensuality. It is beautiful to look at, wonderful to touch, and glorious to wear.

Like any other art form, beadwork is created in context. It reflects a specific time, place, and the aesthetic values of its culture and creator. And it is rooted in prehistory. *The New Beadwork* documents the most recent point on the continuum of this ancient tradition, which dates back thousands of years. And yet, the pieces illustrated in this book were crafted during the past two decades—a period of profound societal change. Most of the artists acknowledge this duality of influence, their deliberate layering of the new upon the traditional. The result is a marvelous body of work that is at once universal and unique, familiar but fresh.

Beadwork is described as "material composed or adorned with beads," with units subordinate to the whole. This differs from strung necklaces, for example, where attention is generally focused on individual beads. And beadwork, unlike gemstone jewelry, is typically constructed of inexpensive glass microbeads, so it has always been valued more for its artistry and craftsmanship than for the intrinsic costliness of its components.

But while the palette of materials is unpretentious, beadwork has frequently been a mark of status, particularly when used in highly stratified societies. Historically, for the Yoruba of Nigeria, the use of heavily beaded materials was a privilege accorded only to kings, their courts, and priests. Among the Cameroon grassland tribes, richly beaded elephant masks literally and visually conveyed wealth and power. In Western cultures, beaded bags and dresses were worn by the well-to-do; they were rarely affordable by working- or poorer-class women.

Tribal beadwork rarely served just as decoration. Rather, it formed an integral part of the culture and rituals for which it was designed. It is also a major source of inspiration for many of the artists featured in this book. One might well ask how contemporary beadworkers, living in Western cultures that seemingly lack relevant traditions from which to derive meaningful symbolic values, manage to create work that is not arbitrary and superficial.

It does not appear to have been a problem for the artists featured in *The New Beadwork*. The authors have selected a superb group of beadworkers, whose work is passionate and has been conceived out of their own experience. Many stress spiritual connections. All have been influenced by and have reacted to the world around them. Although of widely differing aesthetics and backgrounds, the artists have much in common. Each in his or her own way uses beadwork as a means of individual expression. Many of their pieces contain personal messages and symbols concerning the environment and social issues relevant to the late twentieth century. In contrast to the ancient and historic beadworkers who inspired them, these artists are socially conscious within a democratic, antiroyal heritage. Their work is egalitarian. It is, above all, the gift of technically sophisticated artisans, is splendidly crafted, and is based on strong concepts.

Sadly, much historical, ethnographic beadwork is in the marketplace because the culture and its way of life have disintegrated or are in decline. Treasured secular and sacred artifacts have frequently been sold or traded for food, medicine, or transistor radios. In contrast, purchasing contemporary beadwork that has comparable quality and essence allows one to own artistic masterpieces without vandalizing a culture and to support practicing artists at a vital time in their professional lives.

The New Beadwork should change the way people see this timeless art. It is a book about transformation and change, about painting, sculpting, weaving, layering, and building with beads.

Lois Sherr Dubin

KATHLYN MOSS

Captured Light
Beadwork by Contemporary Artists

Imagine light captured in minute fragments of astonishing, luminous color so intricately combined that stained glass seems unwieldy by comparison. Contemporary artists have discovered the power of the tiny glass bead as a medium of light, color, and concept, bursting through the boundaries of traditional, ethnocultural beadwork to create a new art form.

Seed beads are an aggressive art medium. Their glittery surface, their "preciousness," and their sometime association with kitsch can overpower an artistic statement lacking strength. Further, the technical considerations of combining beads with thread or wire to create beadwork present problems inherent in the use of any soft material to support a hard one. Yet many artists have faced the challenges of the medium to create work with spiritual depth and emotional vigor.

A number of today's artists were children in the 1950s and were among those introduced to beadwork through the Girl Scouts, Boy Scouts, Campfire, Inc., and summer craft programs. Since the culture of the Native American was of great interest to these organizations, it was not unusual to find a group of children sitting around a table intently weaving bands of beads on bent-wire bead looms. Often beadwork was used to decorate costumes for reenacting ceremonies derived from Native American customs. For many artists, these childhood experiences of participation in the practices of Native lore, working with bright, sensual glass beads, left a lasting impression.

Instrumental in the teaching of beadwork by these organizations were a number of pamphlets and books. One such book, *American Indian Beadwork*, written in 1951 by W. Ben Hunt and J. F. "Buck" Burshears, originally grew out of the authors' teaching of Native American customs and beadwork to a boy-scout troop in La Junta, Colorado. Other books from this period suggested using imitation seed pearls to make necklaces, earrings, and bracelets based on European designs from the Victorian era. How-to books and pamphlets on knitting and crochet, aimed at the homemaker, included instructions for making simple beaded items such as purses, collars, and cuffs.

The patterns generally called for a single color of seed beads or artificial pearls to be worked into designs derived from various stitches. For many years, this kind of instructional material was the main source of inspiration for beadworkers.

In the early 1960s young people in the United States responded to President John F. Kennedy's call to serve abroad in the Peace Corps. In the program, large numbers of average young Americans traveled the globe, living and working among indigenous peoples of Africa, South America, the South Pacific, and the Indian subcontinent. They were profoundly influenced by the rich cultures of the people they served. For the first time they saw handcrafts, including beadwork, as part of a living culture and not as a collection of artifacts on a shelf in a museum. Returning from their travels, these volunteers brought back souvenirs, including beads and beadwork; more important, they gained a fresh perspective on ways of life that influenced the art-and-craft movement then just beginning.

In the same decade the rock music of the Beatles captured the hearts of European and American youth. In 1967 the Beatles, interested in Eastern religious thought, particularly transcendental meditation, traveled to India to study with the Maharishi Mahesh Yogi. When they returned to England they brought back not only new philosophical ideas, but also a novel way of dressing, including the wearing of beads by men as well as women. Both the religious philosophy and the fashion for "love beads" quickly became popular with their young fans.

During the closing years of the 1960s, the civil-rights movement initiated in the 1950s entered an era of turmoil. Black Americans began to redefine their lives and empower themselves by reclaiming their African heritage. Many began wearing traditional African dress, including trade beads and tribal beadwork. Many journeyed to Africa to rediscover their history and to search for the villages of their forebears. Their interest in African culture spread to other parts of society, and soon many people were collecting old trade beads, masks, baskets, and related art objects.

These social changes combined to create an ardent desire in the nation's youth for a more sensitive and egalitarian way of life. They challenged every institution, including the arts. A new generation of artists began to debate what constituted real art: was it only sculpture, painting, and printmaking—the classic categories of fine art—or could it include other forms of expression, such as those traditionally considered crafts? This debate stimulated artists to create art in nontraditional mediums and energized the field in ways not seen since the advent of modernism.

The influences of the counterculture also were present in Europe, but were driven by a different set of circumstances, mainly those arising from the aftermath of World War II and the fall of colonialism. People from former colonies who immigrated to Europe for work brought their crafts, including beadwork, with them. Also, Victorian beadwork, including beaded purses, dresses, and knickknacks, was still to be found in many homes. In Eastern Europe elaborate beaded embroidery adorned many of the folk costumes still worn for weddings and other celebrations. As in the United States, the presence in Western Europe of disruptive social elements created an atmosphere ripe for experimentation in the arts and traditional crafts, beginning with textiles.

In one of the first major efforts to create an appreciation for textiles as an art form, Jean Lurçat organized the first International Biennial of Tapestry in Lausanne, Switzerland, in 1962. Initially, the primary exhibitors were Europeans, but by the end of the decade artists from North America, Japan, and Australia were also represented. Over the years, textile forms developed from the two- to the three-dimensional and increased in size. The biennial itself grew in prestige and influenced artists who had formerly worked with traditional mediums and techniques. They were fired to explore the application of textiles in the creation of large sculptures. This search for new sculptural forms opened a general investigation into the field of fiber techniques, including beadwork. Simple loom weaving had become passé.

Verena Sieber-Fuchs of Switzerland was one of the artists who had displayed large textile pieces in the biennial.* In 1973 she turned to the more intimate scale of jewelry, crocheting glass and metal seed beads into cords and collars. These beaded jewelry pieces retained the structural focus of her earlier large-scale rope textiles and were constructed with the clean geometric shapes of sculpture. By the mid-1970s Sieber-Fuchs had moved beyond jewelry to pure sculpture, crocheting miniature vessels whose shapes and volumes were amplified by the scintillating reflected light of beaded surfaces.

By the late 1960s, in both Europe and the United States, the flower children, who believed that the power of the earth itself could overcome violence, had inspired groups of people interested in living a simpler life by providing for all their needs through handcrafts and by living in harmony with nature. The hippies emulated those aspects of Native American, African, and Indian cultures they believed had created a more satisfying and spiritually balanced life. Hippies rejected the consumption of the bland, mass-produced products of industrialized America by handcrafting everything from dishes to dwellings. The beadworkers Skip Schuckmann and Annie Buckley, who lived near Golden, Colorado, exemplified this trend. They lived simply in a mountain cabin and sold the crafts they produced for small sums in the belief, common at the time, that it was wrong to earn a profit. They taught beadwork, inspiring many people, while they derived their own inspiration from various sources, Schuckmann from the work of Native Americans, Buckley from European models.

The organic forms and natural themes of the Art Nouveau movement of the nineteenth century held a particular resonance for the hippies in their search for an aesthetic model to guide their ideals. The fantastical architecture of Antonio Gaudi

---

*Works by artists in the text appear in the plates, arranged in alphabetical order by artist's name.

of Spain, with its outlandish curves and rich, almost hallucinogenic surface decoration, inspired much elaborate work in the 1960s. At the same time, some were drawn to the work of the English designer William Morris, who had advocated the use of hand techniques, rather than industrial processes, to create an aesthetically harmonious living environment. Others were captivated by the art of the English Pre-Raphaelites. They recognized a sympathetic vision in paintings of mystical dancing women wearing flowers in their long hair and draped in flowing garments. Like the Pre-Raphaelites, the hippies emphasized high quality in handwork and craftsmanship, in reaction to an increasingly technological society. These art movements had in common an exuberance in the exploration of mediums as well as an attention to detail and balance that energized the hippies in creating their own unique culture.

This interest in handcrafts expressed by the hippies carried over to the art schools, where there was an explosion of creativity in the crafts of ceramics, weaving, jewelry, wood, and glass. In these schools, enthusiasm for crafts resulted in a synthesis of the various craft mediums with traditional art mediums. The art movements of the early twentieth century, with their developments in the use of new materials and images, were of particular interest to students.

One innovation was in the use of collage, which involves combining bits and pieces of paper, wood, and other objects with drawing and painting to create a two-dimensional image. This technique was pioneered in 1912 by the Cubists Georges Braque, Juan Gris, and Pablo Picasso, inspired by the textures, planes, and shapes of African masks and sculpture. The same decade saw the development of assemblage and construction art by the German artist Kurt Schwitters, who arrived at this form of expression through his philosophy of Merz art, which dealt with the products of commerce and industrialization. Collage thus was carried into the third dimension by the juxtaposition of unrelated materials. Dada, founded by Marcel Duchamp and André Breton, among others, continued the development of collage, assemblage, and construction as a critique of the industrial order's effect on society. Anything could be art if viewed in a certain way.

Collage and construction strongly influenced art in the 1960s, particularly the work of Robert Rauschenberg, who incorporated cast-off objects such as old quilts into some of his paintings. In turn, his work inspired art students to try eccentric approaches. These explorations led to the use of mixed mediums—traditional art materials combined with craft techniques and found objects—to express a variety of ideas, from the political to the banal. The Baltimore artist Joyce J. Scott's first collage-and-assemblage neckpieces were constructed with woven yarns, paper, cloth, and ceramics, but none of these materials had the luminescence she enjoyed in glass beads. Her solution was to incorporate plastic, wire, buttons, magazine pictures, and other found objects with beadwork to create narrative pieces about being an African-American and a woman. She says she prefers the hands-on combination of beadwork and mixed mediums to painting, because the latter, with its mess, mixing, and waiting for days for things to dry, is "too much like cooking and cleaning."

By the late 1960s hippies and other counterculture youth were holding festivals and celebrations like those of the cultures they admired. At first these were informal gatherings where old friends could meet, catch up on the past year, and trade handcrafts. Eventually, while retaining their free spirit, these gatherings were organized into craft markets. These "Saturday Markets" became a fixture in several cities, especially on the West Coast. An annual craft fair in Bennington, Vermont, that began twenty-five years ago with craftspeople selling their wares off the tailgates of their pickups has since become the first of the regional craft fairs promoted by American Craft Enterprises, the marketing arm of the American Craft Council. Love beads, simple strands of seed beads, old African trade beads, and beads from India, were a staple of the fairs.

The California jeweler Martin Douglas Kilmer remembers these early years: "I was first introduced to beads by Lucia Antonelli way back when we were playing hippies on the beach in Santa Monica. Lucia was working part-time at a bead store, and that was all it took. First she succumbed and later, when we moved to the woods of northern California, I did. The techniques we used were sewing and stringing, both of which were done to an elaborate degree."

For many, it happened as easily as that. Artists began by collecting a few beads and soon had thousands of the tiny spheres stored in bottles and boxes on shelves or hung in hanks in a rainbow of colors on the wall or in a window. These artists taught themselves techniques from books from the 1950s, and their early experiments often took the form of jewelry, usually necklaces and earrings, as well as small amulet pouches. This first beadwork was rudimentary, made without much consideration for its potential as an art medium, but rather for the pleasure of handling and viewing the beads themselves.

Soon people grew hungry for more information and new books began appearing to fill the need. In 1975 Horace Goodhue, a beadwork enthusiast who had learned various beading techniques from Native Americans all over the United States, published *Indian Bead-Weaving Patterns*, a compilation of many off-loom techniques. This book enabled many artists to expand the range of their work, particularly with netting and peyote stitches. *Simply Beads*, by Betty J. Weber and Anne Duncan, covered basic Native American beadwork techniques and introduced a few from Africa and Mexico. The instructions were accompanied by black-and-white and color photographs of actual pieces from several cultures, suggesting additional design ideas as well as the creative potential of beadwork for more than jewelry.

By now the innovative art forms created with fiber techniques had reached the general public through such museum shows as "Deliberate Entanglements," a traveling exhibition at the University of California, Los Angeles, Galleries in 1971. At the time, the public was also exposed to macrame, and soon this technique was used to make everything from pot hangers to hammocks. Along the way, macrame was combined with beads, thus bringing beadwork further into the realm of sculpture. The interest in macrame was so intense for a few years that dozens of books were written and tons of jute cord and beads imported.

In 1969 Deon DeLange, a beadwork devotee living in Spokane, Washington, saw and admired the beaded earrings of local Native Americans. When she learned that a woman from this group would be teaching a class on beadwork, she signed up and learned to make one earring. DeLange was so fascinated with this beadwork earring that she went on to devise various techniques to make dozens more. Soon she herself was asked to teach.

Teaching led to writing a series of instruction books on beadwork earrings and necklaces. Her first book, *Techniques of Beading Earrings*, published in 1983, was welcomed by many artists who had been searching for more beadworking methods. Soon, at craft fairs around the country, people sold beaded earrings made exactly according to the instructions in her books. DeLange says that she wrote the books in the hope that artists would use them as a source for their own ideas, and is disappointed this has not happened more often. By the late 1980s her earring designs had been copied widely in the sweatshops of Asia for export to the United States.

In 1977 the late Ray C. Davis wrote *Prize Winners: Twelve Loomed Necklaces*, which reintroduced the use of beaded warp threads prevalent in the loomed beadwork necklaces of the 1920s. This book inspired artists to investigate not only the use of beaded warps, but also the addition of supplementary warps and wefts to loom-woven work. Frieda Bates had developed a similar design on her own; Davis's book greatly aided in refining her work, ultimately enabling her to create necklaces of marvelous intricacy. Virginia Blakelock has most fully explored these techniques, weaving elaborate broadcollars and purses. She is particularly adept in the use of a supplementary warp and weft to create additional structural elements, such as the dense fringes that balance the rich visual images in the loomed portion of her work.

In the early 1970s the feminist movement challenged the traditional view of women's work as inferior or subordinate to that of men. All fields were open to reinterpretation, including art, and the notion arose that the traditional feminine pastimes of crocheting, knitting, lace making, quilting, and embroidery could be suitable methods for serious artistic expression. Judy Chicago, through her own creative work in painting and drawing, and by establishing an art program for women at Fresno State College in California, was the first feminist artist and academic to probe these issues. Later this program moved to the Women's Building in Los Angeles, where Chicago was joined by the New York artist Miriam Shapiro, known for her fabric collages.

Chicago and Shapiro encouraged their students to search out and study the work of women artists, such as Mary Cassatt, Georgia O'Keeffe, Louise Nevelson, and Louise Bourgeois. They recommended reading the diaries of Virginia Woolf and Anaïs Nin. These studies, the development of women's-studies programs, and other academic endeavors combined to generate a new point of view in art that focused on the decorated and embellished surface and on female-centered imagery. Women artists felt freer to expand their visual vocabulary from the medium of paint to include beads, buttons, thread, and cloth. At the same time, many found their aesthetic appreciation expanding to encompass quilts, samplers, and beadwork as sources for inspiration.

The philosophies of feminism and various other social-change movements, the aesthetic merits of traditional crafts such as fiber arts, and the concepts of earlier art movements such as Dada and Surrealism finally converged in the late 1970s; from these mixed influences beadwork emerged as a serious art medium. For much of the decade it had remained an avocation for most artists, who continued to pour their creative energies into other art forms, especially painting, weaving, and ceramics. For those making bead jewelry, this was a time for selling work at craft fairs, which had become standardized in the 1970s. These fairs, particularly those sponsored by American Craft Enterprises, were a wonderful forum for the exchange of ideas, spurred by the competition of the marketplace. Howard Newcomb, who made jewelry from porcelain beads he handcrafted, and Ascha Gellman, whose beadwork adorned the leather purses made by her partner, Crow, were among the many artists who developed and refined their work in this environment.

With so many people collecting beads and beadwork, the growing need for information and research became apparent. In Los Angeles in 1974 Robert K. Liu and Carolyn Benesh began to publish *The Bead Journal*, a scholarly research journal. That same year, several of the periodical's subscribers, as well as bead collectors and artists, organized the first bead society in Los Angeles. But while *The Bead Journal* met the needs of researchers and collectors, it did not have as much appeal for artists. Benesh encouraged changes in the magazine's design and format to reach out to these readers. In 1978 *The Bead Journal* became *Ornament*, a magazine dedicated to the art of personal adornment. *Ornament* now features the work of contemporary artists in addition to the writings of bead researchers; it covers everything from jewelry to tattoos, costume, and wearable art, and adornment ancient and modern. This magazine, along with research organizations such as the Center for Bead Research in Lake Placid, New York, and the nearly two dozen bead societies in the United States and Europe, continues to present important information on contemporary and historical beadwork.

By 1978 it occurred to artists—Antonelli, Kilmer, and Carlos Cobos, among others—that beadwork itself offered a legitimate language for expressing dreams, ideas, and images that could not be communicated as well in other art mediums.

Most had made jewelry or other ornamented work as a way of developing an aesthetic for beadwork.

Bead artists who are Native Americans and create work with a contemporary sensibility present a special case. The longtime perception of beadwork as bound by cultural traditions, by Natives and non-Natives alike, has resulted in a barrier to experimentation in creativity that can be troublesome to surmount. Adding to this difficulty is the complexity of straddling two cultures: that of traditional life on the reservation, and that of the modern urban environment. Marcus Amerman is one of a number of artists of Native descent who have transcended this perceptual barrier by drawing on the knowledge and skills taught by their cultural traditions to create exceptional works of art with beads. These artists have a deep respect for their heritage and a desire to overcome the stereotypes and clichés attached to Native American art—not always an easy task.

By the 1980s several artists were using beadwork alone to create astounding works of art, but galleries and museums continued to reject these pieces unless the beadwork was merely an embellishment to a more accepted form, such as painting. Ironically, these same museums and galleries continued to embrace beadwork from Native American and African sources. The former were not considered art; the latter were. At the time, articles on beadwork in art publications were almost nonexistent. What coverage there was usually reported on work considered collage or fiber art, and included beads only incidentally. The fortunate outcome of all this timidity was that artists were left alone to explore the medium of beadwork unhindered by external standards of acceptability, each generally unaware that any other artist might be pursuing similar creative ends. This isolation and official neglect encouraged a greater variety of original work than might have been produced had beadwork received more attention and acceptance. The result is a body of work with an astonishing diversity.

In 1980 the A Gallery in Stinson Beach, California, presented "Beads in Art and Fashion," a show of wearable beadwork curated by the beadworker Robin Cohen. Although the show was little noticed beyond the San Francisco area, it was an inspiration to those who saw it and a validating experience for its participants. The following year saw one of the first museum shows to include contemporary beadwork. "Good as Gold," a traveling show of jewelry fabricated from nontraditional materials, was curated by Lloyd E. Herman, then director of the Renwick Gallery of the Smithsonian Institution in Washington, D.C. This innovative show included a beadwork neckpiece by Joyce Scott called *Snakearms* and a T-necklace, titled *Jazz*, by the California artist Jeanette Ahlgren. "The Bead Goes On," organized in 1987 by the Art Museum of the University of Oregon, Eugene, was the first museum exhibition to focus solely on beadwork as an art medium. It enthralled crowds of people wherever it was shown, and for the first time artists and other art professionals began to regard beadwork as a significant contemporary art form. The University of Oregon exhibition was followed by two more shows: "The Ubiquitous Bead" in the fall of 1987, curated by Ramona Solberg for the Bellevue Art Museum near Seattle, Washington, and "Structure and Surface: Beads in Contemporary American Art," in the winter of 1988, curated by Mark Richard Leach for the John Michael Kohler Art Center in Sheboygan, Wisconsin. Prior to that, the Center for the Study of Beadwork had persuaded the Smithsonian Institution to consider the merits of beadwork as a legitimate art form, and a portion of "Structure and Surface" was reorganized and exhibited at the Renwick Gallery in Washington, D.C., in 1990.

The 1980s also saw the publication of several books with high-quality color photographs of historic and ethnic beadwork. One of the first, *Yoruba Beadwork: Art of Nigeria*, by the Victoria and Albert Museum curator William Fagg, had a major impact on several artists including Donna Wasserstrom. When she came across the book, Wasserstrom knew immediately that she would make beadwork the focus of her art. She was fascinated by the colors, the mix of patterns, and the sculptural quality of the beadwork pieces created by the Yoruba people. Wasserstrom also appreciated the utilitarian aspect of Yoruba art and determined to incorporate these qualities into her own work. In 1984 *Africa Adorned,* by Angela Fisher, was published. This informative book discussed the materials, from paint to beadwork, used by the various tribal groups of the African continent to ornament the body. *Africa Adorned* also inspired artists to expand their view of the potential of beadwork as an expressive medium. Yet another book, *The History of Beads,* by Lois Sherr Dubin, was published in 1987. This was the first comprehensive photographic survey of the history of beads, including beadwork. It introduced the exceptional beading of Indonesia and the Philippines to an appreciative following. All of these books, with their focus on the historic importance of beads and beadwork in the human endeavors of ritual, art, and commerce, were inspirational to many contemporary bead artists seeking to expand the scope of their work.

Artists are especially taken with seed beads because, unlike other beads, they are available in uniform sizes small enough to permit fine graphic detail. The dazzling array of colors and finishes adds to the imaginative possibilities. These attributes enable the bead artist to create works with a depth and complexity of form and light unattainable in any other medium. When Jeanne Leffingwell entered a percent-for-art competition in 1982 to create a sculpture for a large public space in Anchorage, Alaska, her first entry was a series of cloth banners with a touch of bead embroidery. Although the jury liked her work and that of four other artists, they did not consider any of the proposed sculptures appropriate or interesting enough for the space. The panel asked the finalists to try again. After much thought, Leffingwell realized that the most interesting aspect of her work was the beads. She had a flash of inspiration: Why not make a gigantic curtain of strings and strings of beads, with colors like

the northern lights! The finished sculpture, *Sky Curtain,* a shimmering rainbow of color consisting of no less than six miles of strung bugle and seed beads, is a much stronger artistic statement than the first proposal of cloth banners ever could have been. Leffingwell sees beading as an organic building process in which many, many small objects are, with time and patience, built into a surprisingly large and complex whole. Other artists see beadwork as a form of meditation, based on the abstraction of repetition and counting.

Color becomes more than color in glass beads, incorporating all the possibilities of light and glass, from liquid transparency to solid opacity. As Jeannine Goreski notes, "Glass beads are able to transmit light through matter in a way that suggests seeing and entering." She is fascinated by this attribute, which allows her to illuminate a line or shape by placing translucent beads next to opaque ones. The unique opportunity to work with brilliantly colored light attracts many artists with a background in painting. Ahlgren likes the way the processes of her paintings and woven-glass pieces "play against each other, the painting being more active, yet controlled, and the beadwork being more planned, yet wild." The colors in her paintings are gentle and muted, while the "color kinetics" of her beadwork pieces shimmer like butterfly wings. For Jimoh Buraimoh beads have become an extension of the painting process itself. Buraimoh glues opaque seed beads over his paintings to achieve a textured surface like that of sand painting.

Some artists take a minimalist approach to their beadwork, seeking to refine it to the purest expression of geometry and color. In the beadworking process, they strive for simplicity in composition and a balance of line and hue to express more readily the nature of light transmitted through glass beads. These are the considerations the Viennese artist Jacqueline Lillie keeps in mind as she crafts jewelry that is minimalist in texture, color, and shape. She thinks that "the impression created by a piece of jewelry should not be determined by the materials used, but rather by the care invested in its creation and the design selected." Lillie's choice of basic geometric shapes, the square, the circle, and the triangle, coupled with the simplicity of vivid colors, results in jewelry with a strong aesthetic presence.

Any topic may be addressed through the medium of beadwork. Spiritual and political themes are of particular concern for today's artists. The spirituality expressed in the beadwork of Native Americans, Africans, and other traditional cultures has been a revelation to many artists seeking to span the breach between the logic of the intellect and the intuition of the heart—a split that occurred long ago, when the Western world separated reason from spirit. This rupture is mirrored in the separation of the natural from the mechanical world and becomes apparent in the political and sociocultural problems of our times: racism, sexism, a degraded environment, and war.

The purpose of art is spiritual. The artist who seeks to reveal the spiritual uses transformation, magic, and healing. This aspect of art has sometimes been denied in modern times because materialistic cultures are intolerant of ideas that do not fit into a logical, rationalistic model of the universe. Often the spiritual in art is mistakenly associated with the dogma of religion, rather than the universal and sometimes difficult quest for enlightenment that is the real purpose of the artist. Beads and beadwork have long served non-Western cultures in the celebration and recognition of this spiritual journey. Many contemporary bead artists have consciously engaged this journey in their work. Cheri Mossie relates that she finds her designs and colors through prayer and dreams. When she begins a piece, she has no idea what it will look like unless she has already dreamed it. Usually she simply starts beading on a leather panel and soon sees a picture form. Some people say that her work is a form of medicine. Mossie believes this to be true because of the mystical experiences she has while working on a piece and the way the piece always relates to the person who chooses it.

Artists have found that beadwork aids in understanding the spiritual aspects of other cultures. Without planning, some beadworkers find themselves using techniques, colors, and symbols that are part of a universal language. Gretchen Newmark recounts that she once made a little leather pouch decorated with a crescent moon, a star, and a beaded-fringe border to console herself for a death in her family. Shortly after the pouch was completed, she went to see an exhibition of Afro-Brazilian slave-made Mardi Gras costumes from the nineteenth century. She was startled to note that one costume bore the same colors as her pouch, including the same eclectic collection of beads in the identical design of the fringe. She says she felt as if she were seeing her own work, and the experience left her light-headed.

When it comes to social and political considerations, Scott is probably the first artist who used beadwork to narrate her humorous thoughts and acid observations on the ironies of modern life. Her approach to art is multifaceted; she is a performance artist and teacher, as well as a visual artist. Her teaching and her performances provide direct involvement with her audience, and that interaction animates the spiritual and political content of her beadwork. Her sculptural neckpieces, with plump, beaded figures posed in complex narrative tableaux, are intriguing and frequently disturbing. The viewer is enticed past the exterior charms of the work to the realization that it is about serious subjects: love and betrayal, faith and disbelief, virtue and crime, equality, racism, and sexism.

The exciting diversity of the beaded art forms that appeared in the 1980s could only have happened in the fertile atmosphere created by the liberating events of the previous twenty years. Artists have discovered that with seed beads, thread, and glue any concept may be realized, from flat graphic images to fully three-dimensional sculpture. Beadwork may be constructed for the intimate measure of the human body or the grand scale of a public building. It may be for the simple pleasures of adornment and beauty or the loftier goals of instruction and social commentary.

Color, form, intricacy, seduction, and obsession: beadwork has all of these.

The Plates

JEANETTE AHLGREN
Born 1950, Palo Alto, California
Resides in Fortuna, California

Cat Game. 1990. Game board loom-woven
in a single piece and backed with calfskin,
with bead-covered leather game pieces,
30 × 30". Collection the artist

Ahlgren considers this work a "fun" piece. In
it she has utilized as many colors as possible
to develop a complex design of reversing
symmetry, inspired by the works of M. C.
Escher, an artist known for distorting the
fundamentals of perspective.

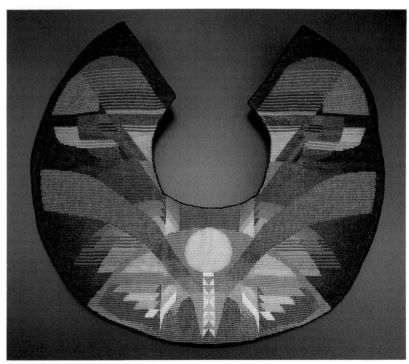

Miles Davis. 1989. Shawl collar loom-woven in a single piece and backed with leather, 19″ diameter; ties (not pictured), 30 × ½″. Collection the artist

Ahlgren designed this piece to initiate a large new loom constructed by her husband. The size of the loom allowed her to move beyond the constraints of the rectangle to weave her first circular work. The colors and imagery in this collar were inspired by the classical jazz abstractions of Miles Davis.

Jazz. 1981. T-necklace loom-woven in two sections and assembled with leather backing, neckband, 2 × 15½″; body, 20 × 5″. Collection D. R. Bibby, Fortuna, California

A painter, Ahlgren is fascinated by the blending of colors to achieve subtle gradations and optical illusions. To achieve these effects in beadwork, she has developed a beading technique she calls the "random-dot bleed pattern," a method of blending colors. Her use of muted colors in the background and brighter tones in the foreground produces painterly images that appear three-dimensional. Ahlgren depicts themes from her daily life, such as the family cat marching through the landscape in this necklace.

MARCUS AMERMAN
Born 1959, Phoenix, Arizona
Resides in Santa Fe, New Mexico

ABOVE:

Red Shirt. 1988. Wallpiece of seed-bead embroidery in various stitches on cotton, 9 × 7". Collection Misa Joo, Eugene, Oregon

Amerman, of Choctaw descent, received extended family instruction, beginning in childhood, in the production of decorative and ceremonial beaded regalia. He uses these early creative influences, as well as formal art-school training, to inform work that moves beyond traditional Native American expression, while the subject matter of his images amplifies and honors his heritage. His beadwork focuses on photorealist images, based on early black-and-white photographs of Native heroes who fought and died for their families and the future of their way of life. Wanting to create something beautiful for their descendants, Amerman sews beads in arcs and sweeps to intensify the depth of his images and the richness of his colors, adding to the sense of realism.

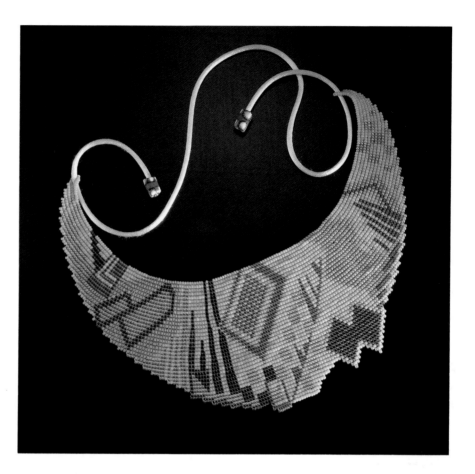

OPPOSITE:

Trailing-the-Enemy and His Wife. 1988. Wallpiece of seed-bead embroidery in various stitches on cotton, 10⅜ × 6⅞″. Collection Marti Root, Phoenix, Oregon

Amerman created this piece, the last in a series of pictorials illuminating the heroes of the Kiowa nation, for a show at the Southern Plains Indian Museum in Anadarko, Oklahoma. He says he envisions this series as displayed with the brave stories of the subjects, told in their own words, beside each portrait.

HANNE SUE ANAYA
Born 1948, Heiligenhafen, Germany
Resides in Arcosanti, Arizona

ABOVE RIGHT:

Green Peace. 1988. Neckpiece woven in square stitch, 8 × 12″. Collection the artist

Anaya began this piece after finding seed beads in a light green that spoke to her of the healing power of nature. She works intuitively, adding colors to her compositions until symbols begin to emerge. At this point she becomes conscious of the story being created by her hands. Here, the artist has used the tug of complementary colors to tell a parable about the friction inherent in humanity's desire for both nature and civilization.

RIGHT:

The Magus. 1990. Cuff woven in square stitch, 4 × 8″ circumference. Collection the artist

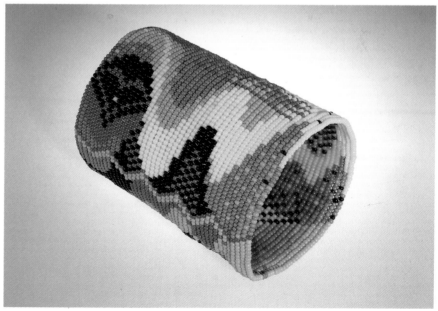

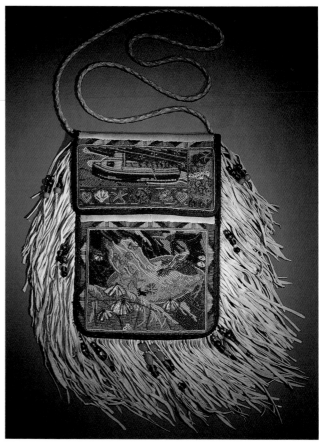

SUSAN ANNISKETT
Born 1956, Pensacola, Florida
Resides in Haines, Alaska

Spirit Horses Wall Pocket. 1985. Folded and stitched leather bag with bead embroidery and attached fringe, 18 × 12 × ½". Collection Roland W. Crawford, Objects of Bright Pride Gallery, New York City

In this work Anniskett examines the contrasts between traditional Native American geometric designs and "realistic" images. She creates visual energy through the use of diagonal lines and by playing the movement of the horses against the static geometry of the background.

Tidal Pool Bag: A Tribute to Prince William Sound. 1989. Diptych of bead embroidery on handcrafted bag of Sitka deerhide with old trade-bead accents, 12 × 8 × ½". Collection Tsutomu Sanada, Hiroshima, Japan

Anniskett, living in Cordova, Alaska, at the time of the disastrous 1989 oil spill in Prince William Sound, began this bag the following day. Having witnessed the devastation first-hand, she was moved to portray the sound before the spill. Her designs have been inspired by her life among Native Americans, beaded bags seen in antique shops, and the beaded trim her grandmother sewed to dresses. Anniskett sees her own artworks as heirlooms to be passed to future generations.

LUCIA ANTONELLI
Born 1947, Endicott, New York
Resides in Petaluma, California

Fire Rising. 1990. Neckpiece with antique silver-and-carnelian buckle from Sri Lanka stitched to leather, framed with metal seed beads, secured with lazy stitch, and finished with strung and braided glass and metal seed beads, Kenyan brass *heishi*, and semi-precious stones, $24 \times 3 \times \frac{1}{2}''$. Collection the artist

Antonelli loves to produce jewelry that, in her words, "at first glance looks as though it came from another place and time." She collects beads, talismans, and ritual objects from other cultures as well as the work of contemporary artists to use as focal points in her adornments. She respects and identifies with the creative spirit of these other artists when she combines the products of their hands with her own artistic efforts. Antonelli employs basic techniques such as stringing, sewing, and braiding in elaborate ways, creating the repetition of line, color, and texture that gives her jewelry its sensual movement and vitality.

See also COLLABORATION

ANN BAILEY
Born 1959, Medford, Massachusetts
Resides in Lincoln, Nebraska

Dancing in the Sun. 1990. Collar embroidered with bugle and seed beads on vinyl fabric with cotton streamers, 49 × 49", from streamer end to streamer end. Collection the artist

Bailey spent two years embroidering this piece, stitching a few beads at a time, working through each section of the collar. Her inspiration came from African creation myths about the sun as the source of life. Her use of both bugle and seed beads emphasizes the brilliance and liveliness of the colors and the radiating movement achieved by the repetition of similar design elements.

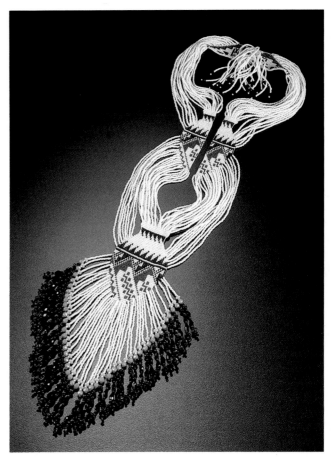

CAROLYN PRINCE BATCHELOR
Born 1941, Tallahassee, Florida
Resides in Upland, California

Rahel. 1990. Sculpture of hand-rolled, painted paper beads sewn to a paper form and mounted on a Plexiglas stand, $9\frac{1}{2} \times 9\frac{1}{2} \times 1''$. Collection the artist

Batchelor hand-rolls paper beads because they may be made to resemble other materials, such as bone or glass, and because of a fascination with art related to childhood experiences. Her works are conceptual pieces that take the form of symbolic garments, which she sees as stand-ins for the absent wearers. She views these garments as having power similar to that possessed by tribal beaded and quilled clothing.

FRIEDA BATES
Born 1950, Tillamook, Oregon
Resides in Artesia, New Mexico

Timeless. 1989. Necklace loom-woven in a technique of beaded floating warps, finished with fire-polished glass crystals and seed-bead fringe, $22 \times 2\frac{1}{8}''$. Collection the artist

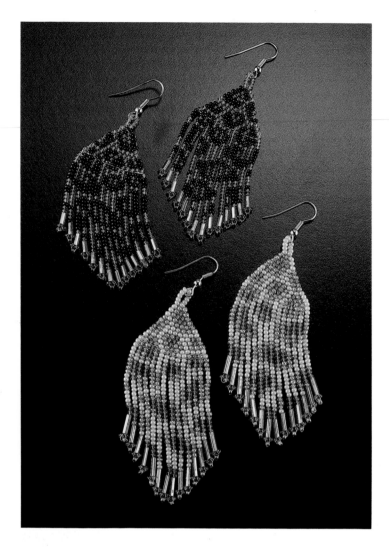

LORI BERRY
Born 1955, Van Nuys, California
Resides in San Pablo, California

Leopard Spots. 1987. Two pairs of earrings in brick stitch with attached fringe, each $3\frac{1}{2} \times 2''$. Collection the artist

Berry has woven a "spirit bead" of an unmatching color and style into each earring. The significance of this bead pertains to the ancient tradition of Navajo weavers, who wove a spirit path into their weavings so that the spirit of the weaver would not become trapped in the work.

ELIZABETH BERTUCCIO
Born 1958, Cleveland, Ohio
Resides in Portland, Oregon

OPPOSITE TOP:

Eyed Hawk Moth. 1989. Scarf slide of loom-woven seed beads, $1 \times 2\frac{1}{2}''$. Collection the artist

Bertuccio is captivated by images of birds, butterflies, and flowers, and the other denizens of the natural world. For the artist, each brooch or pair of earrings is a meditation on the environment; her art is an effort to comprehend and reveal nature.

OPPOSITE LEFT:

Viceroy Butterflies. 1989. Earrings of loom-woven seed beads with handmade silver ear wires, $2 \times 1''$. Collection Center for the Study of Beadwork, Portland, Oregon

OPPOSITE RIGHT:

Eastern Parrots. 1990. Earrings loom-woven of antique size 20° seed beads, with handmade silver ear wires, each $1\frac{1}{2}'' \times \frac{1}{2}''$. Collection the artist

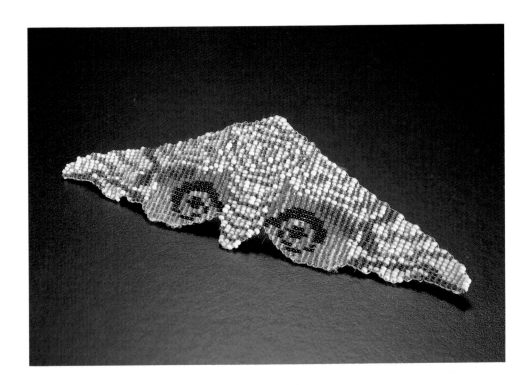

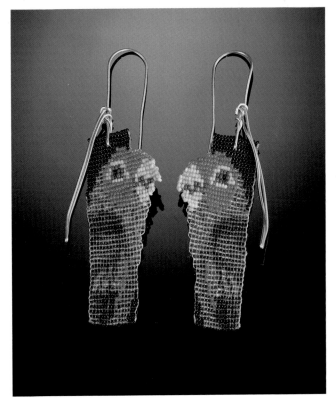

JOHN BINZLEY
Born 1955, Santa Barbara, California
Resides in Jerome, Arizona, and Bali

Desert Night. 1977. Neckpiece with bottle, worked with charlotte beads in peyote stitch (Native American variation), lapis lazuli, amber, carnelian, agate, cut glass, and silver, 13 × 6½ × 1". Collection the artist

Green Medicine Bag. 1979. Bag of deer-hide appliquéd with charlotte beads in tubular and flat peyote stitch (Native American variation), with a green-turquoise-and-silver medallion, 12 × 7". Collection the artist

Binzley states that the beadwork motifs in this bag illustrate a personal symbolism representing the story of the soul from birth to death. The soul begins its journey in the designs at the bottom of the bag, rising through the rainbow-colored sections to the black-and-white designs in the middle. These black-and-white patterns represent life's opposing forces.

VIRGINIA BLAKELOCK
Born 1952, Dayton, Ohio
Resides in Wilsonville, Oregon

Daphnis Nerii. 1985. Necklace of loomwork with supplementary warp and off-loom techniques, 16 × 10". Collection the artist

When her work contains a pictorial image, Blakelock begins by charting the image in black and white. She improvises color around a basic scheme developed before she starts to weave. For this piece she redrew graphs and started weaving twice before she got the colors and proportions of the moth just right. She ingeniously solved the problem of what to do with hundreds of loose warp ends by making lots of fringe and weaving extra ends into the structure of the collar itself. Still, for Blakelock, fringe is more than just something to do with extra thread; with it she elaborates the overall design by stringing beads that both reflect and amplify the color pattern in the body of the neckpiece.

Crude Root. 1988. Neckpiece of loomwork, peyote stitch, bead embroidery, and branched fringe, with steel and cut-glass beads, 16 × 9 × 2½". Collection the artist

This piece started out as a woven sampler for one of Blakelock's beadwork classes and remained unresolved until a colleague told her about a technique seen on a Pakistani belly dancer's costume. The technique was a form of feathery fringe featuring branches jutting out in all directions. The piece is wonderfully organic and erotically suggestive.

FLORA BOOK
Born 1926, Perth Amboy,
New Jersey
Resides in Seattle, Washington

Birds I. 1986. Necklace of 4-mm sterling-silver beads woven on nylon monofilament, $24 \times 19''$. Collection the artist

With this piece Book wanted to create a garment both soft and flowing, using the human body as its armature. The necklace, or garment, drapes over the front and back of the wearer, who, as he or she moves, causes the beads to slide back and forth on their filaments, creating patterns reminiscent of a flock of birds in flight.

JOE BOWMAN
Born 1954, Birlington, Wisconsin
Resides in Sandpoint, Idaho

Sacred Ground. 1988. Ceremonial fan of turkey feathers constructed in the manner of the Oglala Sioux, with wood substructure covered in peyote stitch (Native American variation) and a plume of horsehair, $47 \times 13 \times 1\frac{1}{2}''$. Collection the artist

Bowman's choice to make a ceremonial fan with a cross-shaped handle arose from a desire to understand the influence of missionaries on Native American beliefs and ceremonies. The cross is a difficult structure, representing opposing forces. Bowman uses the patterns and colors to unify the push and pull of these contradictory elements.

KATE BOYAN
Born 1956, Banning, California
Resides in Anchorage, Alaska

Money Monster Versus Nature. 1989. Wallpiece of bead-embroidered appliqué on smoked moosehide, 24 × 42 × 1½″. Collection the artist

Like her colleague Susan Anniskett, Boyan was living in Cordova, Alaska, at the time of the Prince William Sound oil spill in 1989. In this narrative work the artist uses a gas-guzzling car speeding down the highway as a symbol for our culture's reliance on oil. The whale floating in the sky and the dead animals and birds are symbolic of the price the environment pays in order for humans to secure the fuel that drives our society.

JIMOH BURAIMOH
Born in Oshogbo, Nigeria
Resides in Oshogbo, Nigeria

Bata Drummers. 1985. Painting on plywood with beads, both loose and strung, glued over the image, 36 × 24 × ¼″. Collection Center for the Study of Beadwork, Portland, Oregon

Coming out of the Mbari Artists Club in Oshogbo, Nigeria, Buraimoh is one of the original artists who worked and studied with Ulli Beier in the mid-1960s. He originated his style of bead painting partly as a nod to mosaics, and also as a way of setting his work apart from that of other painters. His flowing designs, hovering on the boundary between realism and abstraction, are instantly recog-

nizable. This work is a portrait of Bata drummers, or festival players. Four instruments make up a set of Bata drums. The smallest are the *Omele Ako*, which gives the high tone, and *Omele Abo*, which gives a soft tone. They are bound together and are always played by one person. *Iya Ily* is the "talking drum" that leads the others, and *Ome Agba*, not visible, is next to it.

MICHAEL VAN CHAPMAN
Born 1952, Kansas City, Missouri
Resides in Ester, Alaska

ABOVE:

Brooch. 1987. Ornament of appliqué on felt of size 24° seed beads with amethyst centerpiece, surrounded by emeralds and lapis lazuli, 2 × 2". Collection Ruby Moon, Corvallis, Oregon

DAVID CHATT
Born 1960, Sedro Woolley, Washington
Resides in Seattle, Washington

OPPOSITE:

Vase. 1990. Glass vessel covered with seed beads in peyote stitch, 8 × 5" diameter. Collection the artist

Chatt is interested in the aesthetic effects of color and texture on form. Having worked with clay and silver for several years, he finds he prefers to use glass beads to build shapes of rare, luminous color with unusual textures. He relishes the "wonderful tedium of detail" inherent in creating with beads.

ROBERT BURNINGHAM
Born 1920, Saint Paul, Minnesota
Resides in Saint Paul, Minnesota

Three Birds. 1985. Wallpiece in cotton and silk-fiber stitchery with metallic threadwork and beads on cotton, 24 × 24". Collection the artist

CARLOS COBOS

Born 1947, Austin, Texas
Resides in Santa Fe, New Mexico

John Brown. 1974. Wallpiece of couched beadwork on canvas with buttons, 12 × 12". Collection Peter Dare, Myersville, Maryland

Cobos has been creating his beaded works, which he calls beadings, for twenty-five years. This piece, named for the man who guided him in his first year of university teaching, is an early work from a continuing narrative series. The artist works intuitively, beginning with a circular shape formed by a hoop that holds the fabric backing. The design may be figurative or abstract, depending on the events in the artist's life at the time of its creation. Figurative work usually follows a period in which he has made abstract compositions.

To begin a piece, Cobos chooses a palette based on three key colors. One of these colors is carried over from the preceding artwork, thus forming a bridge between pieces. The artist carries a particular three-color palette through three compositions. When he completes a beading, he examines the results and picks the strongest elements for incorporation in the next one. He is fascinated by the process of using tiny elements, particularly such little round "things" as seed beads and dabs of paint, to create a larger picture. These same elements are vital to his paintings and photographs, composed of spots of light or dots of paint.

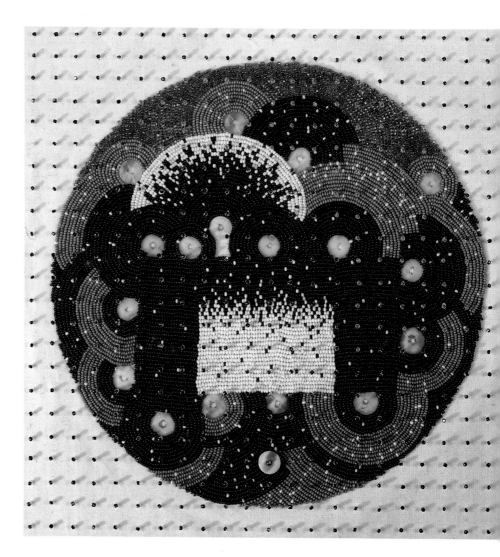

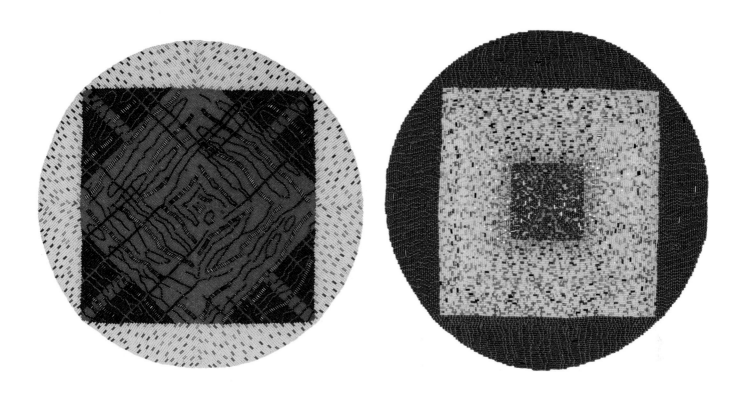

Falling Out. 1990. Wallpiece of couched beadwork on canvas, 16 × 16 × 1¼″. Collection the artist

While the colors and pictorial elements of this work are very different from those in *John Brown*, it is a direct descendant of that earlier piece. If it were possible to line up all the artist's beadings together, the relationship and narrative direction from one to the next would be clear.

This is the first beading completed by Cobos after a move to Santa Fe, New Mex-ico. The red and blue in the central square are colors the artist had been using in his previous residence, in Washington, D.C. Cobos says his intuition led him to choose yellow as the third color because its liveliness seemed appropriate to his new home. This particular piece also has a movement and dynamism unusual in Cobos's work.

Dayaks. 1990. Wallpiece of couched bead-work on canvas, 16 × 16 × 1¼″. Collection Josephine Gamez, San Antonio, Texas

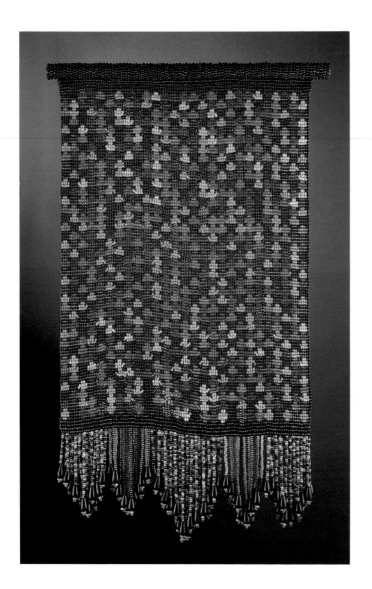

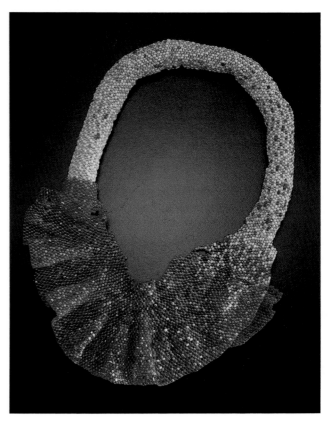

EVELYN COHEN
Born 1954, Surrey, England
Resides in Coombes, West Sussex,
England

Blue Mood. 1985. Wall or window hanging of loom-woven seed beads mounted on wood dowel, 18½ × 11½". Collection the artist

TERESA COLE
Born 1961, Athens, Georgia
Resides in Tallahassee, Florida

Sea Slug. 1985. Collar in flat and tubular peyote-stitch techniques, 8 × 6 × ½". Collection the artist

Cole creates plump, wearable sculpture with a strong organic nature. The shadings of color and the thick free-form tube with pleated ruff readily bring to mind the sea creature for which this collar is titled.

COLLABORATION

Blue Sky Kimono. 1982. Neckpiece with enamel plaque by Laura Popenoe, in cloisonné with gold and silver inlays and an overlay of electroformed copper motifs, backed with leather and framed with sewn and strung beadwork designed by Lucia Antonelli and executed by Martin Douglas Kilmer, 24 × 5″. Collection Martin Douglas Kilmer, Petaluma, California

A singularly successful collaborative relationship began in the fall of 1981, when Laura Popenoe, an expert enamalist, approached Martin Douglas Kilmer and Lucia Antonelli at the Mill Valley Arts Festival, and asked if they would create a necklace with one of her enamels, in exchange for a piece of her work. Kilmer and Antonelli readily agreed and a new partnership was born. It produced a series of necklaces, each possessing a beauty beyond that of mere adornment and an almost mythic or talismanic power. This relationship, formally called Collaboration, lasted until 1986, when the artists returned to producing individual work. Occasionally they still create objects together. For all three, the goal of Collaboration was to take bead stringing to its ultimate conclusion by framing and enhancing the enamel focal point, thus achieving a unity not only among artists, but among diverse materials.

DEON DELANGE
Born 1938, Salt Lake City, Utah
Resides in Waldport, Oregon

Earrings. 1990. Three pairs of earrings in brick stitch and other stringing techniques, average size, each earring, 2½×¾". Collection the artist

These examples of DeLange's work display techniques popularized in her beaded-earring books.

EDWARD DERWENT
Born 1952, Freeport, Illinois
Resides in Chicago, Illinois

OPPOSITE:

Purgatory (detail). 1985–86. Monumental bead tapestry of size 10° seed beads loom-woven in sixteen-inch-wide strips and assembled, 84×54". Collection the artist

Derwent tackled a true challenge when he wove this large beaded work, which recalls the wall tapestries of medieval Europe. Inspired by Dante's *Divine Comedy*, he sketched a series of thought-provoking portraits of human folly to serve as cartoons for his weaving. While his well-executed images would be powerful as paintings, they are transcendent when rendered on this scale in beads. This work is the first in a series and the most colorful. With its bright tones, mythological symbols, skeletons, and collection of tortured humans symmetrically composed within a flattened perspective, the tapestry is reminiscent of the retablos or devotional art of Mexico or Tibetan tankas.

AS THEY PURSUED THE EVER-SHIFTING ILLUSION OF THEIR OWN ADVANTAGE, SO THEY PURSUE ETERNALLY AN ELUSIVE, EVER-CHANGING CONCORD.

MARY DICKEY

Born 1946, Sturgeon Bay, Wisconsin
Resides in Sauk City, Wisconsin

<small>ABOVE:</small>

Wedding Pin for Irene. 1982. Pin of a loom-woven strip with glass and metal beads, cast-silver seed pods, and a handmade sterling-silver finding, $6 \times 3\frac{1}{2} \times 2\frac{1}{2}$″. Collection Irene Dickey, Manhasset, New York

MARY DICKEY

Primordial Stew. 1986. Neckpiece of loom-woven beadwork with crocheted edges, incorporating shells, seed beads, silver beads, ostrich-eggshell beads, brass, and coral, with knotting and folding, finished with a hand-made sterling-silver finding, 8½ × 5 × 1". Collection the artist

M. K. DILLI
Born 1936, Baltimore, Maryland
Resides in Baltimore, Maryland

Two-Way Red Necklace. 1985. Necklace with detachable snakeskin brooch in peyote stitch with supplementary bead embroidery, 12½ × 8½ × ¼". Collection Rosemary K. Dilli, Baltimore, Maryland

ANGELA GAUTHIER
Born 1950, Seattle, Washington
Resides in Everett, Washington

Earrings. 1990. Two pairs of earrings of seed beads and semiprecious stones, embroidered on Ultrasuede and appliquéd to leather backing, with gemstone dangles, each c. 2 × ¾". Collection the artist

Gauthier's portrayal of natural scenes has been influenced by the organic, flowing lines and balanced compositions of Art Nouveau. Her use of color is precise and harmonious, lending the images of birds she often uses a sense of poised serenity. The placement and direction of the lines of beads, so essential to the image, display Gauthier's skill with the needle and her attention to detail.

Double Wood Duck Pendant. 1985. Necklace of seed beads embroidered on felt and appliquéd to leather backing, with braided-leather neck straps covered in peyote stitch, 8 × 2¾ × ¼". Collection Roberta Montana, Seattle, Washington

ASCHA GELLMAN
Born 1956, Los Angeles, California
Resides in Redway, California

Medicine Bag. 1989. Handbag of cowhide by Crow, with embroidered mandala of seed beads and semiprecious stones and a handmade silver centerpiece, 16 × 9 × ¾"; mandala, 3¼" diameter. Collection the artist

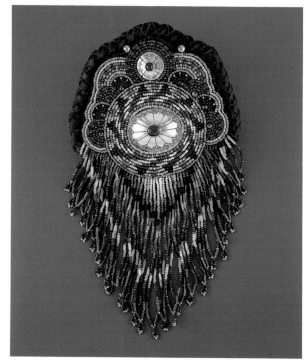

Heavy Blue. 1990. Pendant of bead embroidery appliquéd on leather with silver and lapis-lazuli focal points and braided-leather neckpiece (not pictured), leatherwork by Crow, 8 × 5 × ½". Collection the artist

JEANNINE GORESKI
Born 1956, Chicago, Illinois
Resides in Berthoud, Colorado

Red Bowl. 1988. Vessel of seed beads and nylon thread in brick stitch, $2\frac{1}{2} \times 4''$ diameter. Collection Sanford Besser, Little Rock, Arkansas

Goreski makes bead vessels, which she sees as full, containing "vastness, energy, subtleties, memories, and questions." Yet these vessels are also empty, offering stillness. The center of a vessel, "crucial both structurally and philosophically, is the genesis from which the container spirals outward and upward." Stitched together, beads lock into an orderly brick pattern, formalizing discrete passages of light and color. Here, Goreski uses touches of other colors to denote changes in time and direction through the four quadrants.

Vulnerary. 1985. Sculpture of bottle covered with brick-stitched beadwork and loom-woven bag, $2\frac{1}{2} \times 4\frac{1}{2} \times 3''$. Collection John Goreski, Berthoud, Colorado

Goreski uses the bottle to embody the idea of a healing potion or elixir. One side of the bottle is decorated with an empty triangle, representing loss; on the other is a full triangle, symbolizing renewal. The colorful, quiltlike imagery of the bag refers to comfort, protection, and nurturing.

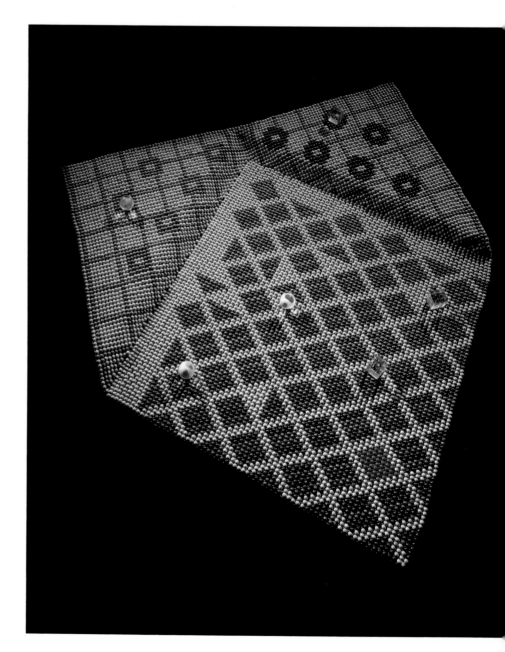

MARY OWEN GRIFFIN
Born 1951, Seattle, Washington
Resides in Olympia, Washington

___

U Do It Art: Gameboard. 1983. Sculptural game board of hand-dyed wood beads assembled with thread in the artist's version of square stitch, with Plexiglas game pieces, $26 \times 22 \times \frac{3}{4}''$. Collection the artist

Griffin creates sculptures on a grand scale that challenge the viewer's assumptions about beadwork. In her work she addresses the plane of the surface as well as underlying structure. With this game board she asks the onlooker to take up the game pieces and become a participant in the creation of art.

SHERRY HART
Born 1949, Denver, Colorado
Resides in Boulder, Colorado

LEFT:

In Light and Mint. 1987. Sculpture of a lantern covered with strung seed beads glued in place, $16 \times 8\frac{1}{2} \times 6\frac{1}{2}$". Collection Bruce W. Hart, McKinleyville, California

In this sculpture, Hart intends a play on words and symbols. "Two snakes rise from a bed of mint leaves to face each other over the place where the flame rises. A rainbow curves around this opening. The Eye knows the invisible flame, the spark of knowledge. The lantern, a symbol for seeing in the Dark, was itself the inspiration for this piece."

MARY HAYSLIP
Born 1954, Houston, Texas
Resides in Houston, Texas

ABOVE:

Sacred Heart. 1985. Pin of seed-bead-and-sequin appliqué on felt, $2 \times 3 \times \frac{1}{8}$". Courtesy Artwear, New York City, collection the artist

VALERIE HECTOR
Born 1960, Evanston, Illinois
Resides in Chicago, Illinois

Bracelet for Anna Akhmatova. 1990. Cuff of strung sterling-silver and glass seed beads wrapped, layered, and glued over wood links, staggered to allow each component to mesh easily, finished with a sterling-silver clasp, $3 \times 8 \times \frac{1}{2}''$. Collection the artist

Hector created a series of bracelets based on her investigations into the concentric stacking of single beaded strands. She made these experimental pieces in an effort to discover how many layers were possible before such a linked structure would no longer function.

Anemone Necklace #4: Lavender and Mint. 1989. Necklace of identical components attached to an Ultrasuede backing; each component fabricated of rows of strung beads glued over a wood core, with fringe and trim sewn into the core; cord ends are bead-covered wood cones capped in oxidized sterling silver, $12\frac{1}{2} \times 11\frac{1}{4} \times \frac{1}{2}''$. Collection the artist

Hector is captivated by the beadwork of Indonesia. This necklace was inspired by the *sessak*, a dancer's fringed girdle made by the people of Celebes. Here she explores the capacity of fringe to impart movement and fullness by repeating a simple design component. Hector's use of colors that are split complements adds to the illusion of motion. The artist strives to create works that are visually rich and harmonious, while maintaining an economy of form.

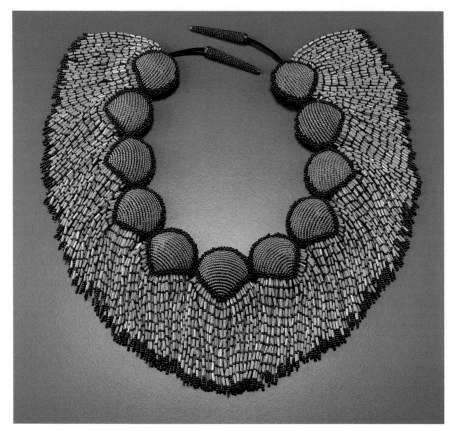

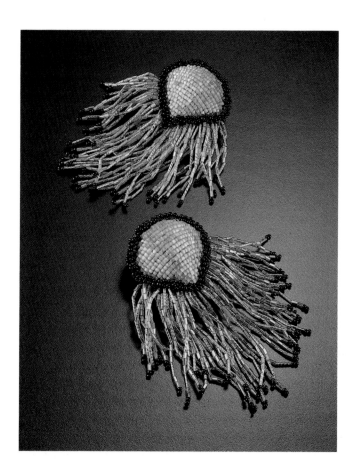

Nefertiti Earrings. 1989. Earrings of rows of strung seed beads glued over a wood core, with bead trim and fringe sewn into wood core, each 3½ × 2½ × ½". Collection the artist

These earrings are part of Hector's Anemone series, which explores the idea of graceful, flowing form as inspired by the sea creature's vividly colored, undulating tentacles.

Potala. 1990. Brooch or wall ornament comprising a cast sterling-silver element with pin, a central support of strung seed beads wrapped, layered, and glued to wood, and tassels of size 18° to 24° beads, with some strands woven in right-angle technique, 9 × 5 × ½". Collection the artist

This work is Hector's tribute to Alexandra David-Neel, a passionate explorer of remot-

est Asia and scholar of Buddhist spirituality who trekked to the forbidden city of Lhasa, Tibet, where she climbed to the top of the Potala Palace. Each tassel of this piece contains one strand of beadwork differing from the others, to represent the path of enlightenment. Complementary colors in the tassels create a note of asymmetry within a symmetrical structure, inviting contemplation of the multiple meanings within the work.

MARY B. HETZ
Born 1949, Des Moines, Iowa
Resides in Solana Beach, California

Bird Collar. 1990. Necklace of wire-strung seed beads wrapped and glued over a shaped leather form, finished with fringe sewn along the edge of the form, 9½ × 7". Collection the artist

OPPOSITE TOP:

Snake. 1989. Belt of wire-strung glass beads wrapped and glued over a shaped leather form, 2½ × 32". Collection the artist

Hetz's interest in animals and wildlife preservation is apparent in the figurative imagery of her beaded fashion accessories. She made her first belt in 1981, when she realized that by placing vertical lines of beads side by side in short, dense rows she could create any likeness she desired on a leather panel. Soon she discovered that by cutting the leather base into the contour of an animal she strengthened the imagery created with the beads.

OPPOSITE LEFT:

Tiger. 1989. Belt of wire-strung seed beads wrapped and glued over a shaped leather form, 2½ × 32". Collection the artist

Through the careful use of color and design, Hetz creates a sharply defined, naturalistic image that evokes the spirit of the animal, as portrayed in the totems of aboriginal people.

OPPOSITE RIGHT:

Eagle. 1990. Belt of wire-strung seed beads wrapped and glued over a shaped leather form, 2½ × 32". Collection the artist

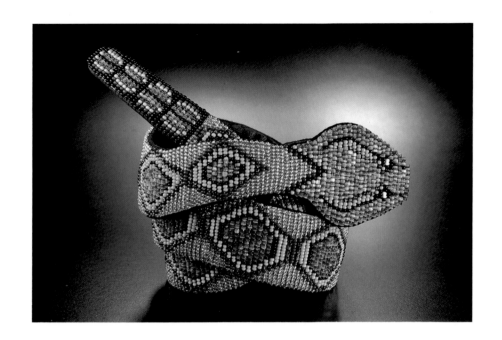

MARY ANN HICKEY
Born 1936, Chicago, Illinois
Resides in Chicago, Illinois

Return to the Goddess. 1989–90. Wall-piece of seed-bead and thread embroidery on a photocopy image heat-transferred to satin, mounted on wood upholstered in Ultrasuede, 11 × 11¾ × 1¼". Collection the artist

This piece is the last in a series of self-portraits depicting Hickey in her bridal gown more than thirty years and thirty pounds after her wedding. Trying on the gown generated in her a spiritual experience that led her to an artistic exploration she calls the Outgrown series. The gown, both metaphorically and physically outgrown, became a personal symbol for private, social, and institutional change. Raised a Catholic, Hickey was ac-customed to seeing altarpieces, icons, and reliquaries. Her gradual assimilation of feminist ideals led her to appreciate women's spirituality and made her aware of a goddess principle that she finds more comforting than the notion of a patriarchal god. In reading widely on this subject, Hickey has come to understand the devotion to the Blessed Virgin in early Christianity as the church's attempt to appease its newest converts, reluctant to abandon their goddess. She views her own artworks as reliquaries of the memory of women's lives subjugated by patriarchy. She uses beads to depict images of the ancient goddess in red, gray, and brown tones that represent the minerals of the earth and the blood of life, and also incorporates colors that echo the brilliance and sparkle of Byzantine mosaics.

MIMI HOLMES
Born 1956, New Orleans, Louisiana
Resides in Mount Vernon, Iowa

OPPOSITE:

Heart's Desire. 1987. Rattle sculpture of fiberfill and seed-bead-embroidered muslin over a wire armature, incorporating a condom, a plastic heart, shells, wood beads, and nickel-silver clappers, 5½ × 2 × 1½". Collection the artist

Holmes sews beads one, two, three, or four at a time, using backstitch. To begin a work, she spends time sketching until she discovers a form that intrigues her. She works out the pattern and colors of the beading in detail, to avoid having to rip out and redo hours of work. Only when her plans are clear and complete does she begin beading, using not only a variety of beads, but also found objects of all sorts.

After a residency at Blue Mountain Center in upstate New York in 1986, Holmes began to make little figures in the form of a paleolithic fertility goddess, of a size to fit the hand, and these became increasingly intimate in spirit. *Heart's Desire* is one such figure, but it also alludes to insects or pupae, in the bronze color of its beaded carapace and its cocoonlike shape, with a cluster of dried-up eggs on the belly. The egg cluster is an image of fertility and, for the artist, a personal emblem of creativity; in its desiccated form it signifies that actually achieving one's heart's desire is not always a good thing; striving for the goal may be more enjoyable—and indeed important—than reaching it.

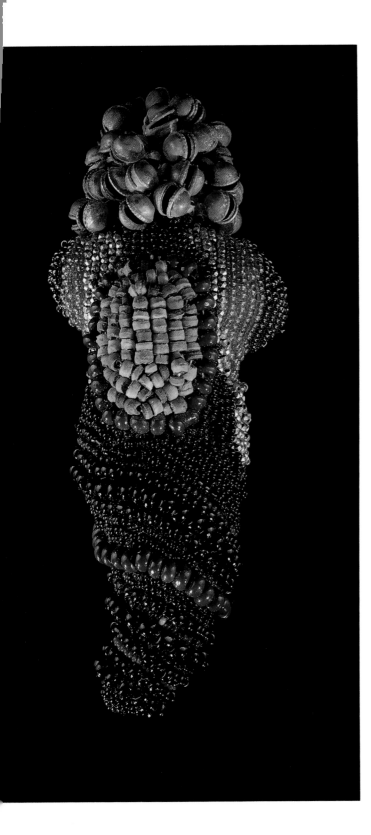

EDGAR JACKSON
Resides on Fort Hall Indian
Reservation, Idaho

ABOVE

Buffalo Hunt. c. 1988. Purse of bead embroidery on pellon sewn to leather backing, with leather straps covered with seed beads in peyote stitch, 10" diameter × 1¾". Collection Frieda Bates, Artesia, New Mexico

Jackson belongs to the Shoshone tribe and pursues a traditional life on the Fort Hall Reservation near Pocatello, Idaho. He brings a refined sense of color and composition to the designs he beads on bags formed in the classic shape of a canteen. He favors the use of a large area of strong color to balance and contain the dynamic intensity of his images.

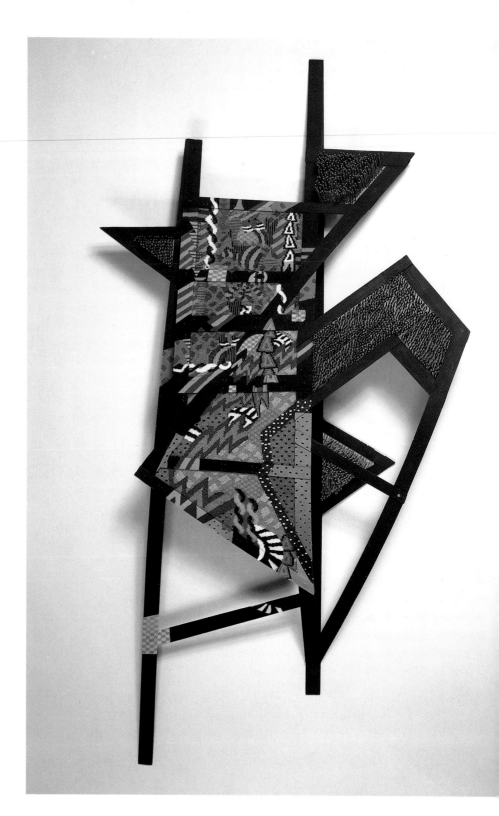

PEGGY KENDELLEN
Born 1952, Milwaukee, Wisconsin
Resides in Portland, Oregon

In the Daring Night. 1990. Sculpture of painted-wood lattice with loom-woven bead panels stitched to the lattice, $57 \times 33 \times 7''$. Collection the artist

Inspired by a Yoruba beaded royal tunic worn by a thunder-god-possession priest, this shieldlike work symbolizes power and protection. It also encompasses the notion of opposites: the beadwork represents an inner, contemplative process, while the textured stickwork exhibits an aggressive, outer-directed sensibility. On a deeper level, Kendellen's work is also about the devices people use to protect themselves: shields, scaffolding, clothing.

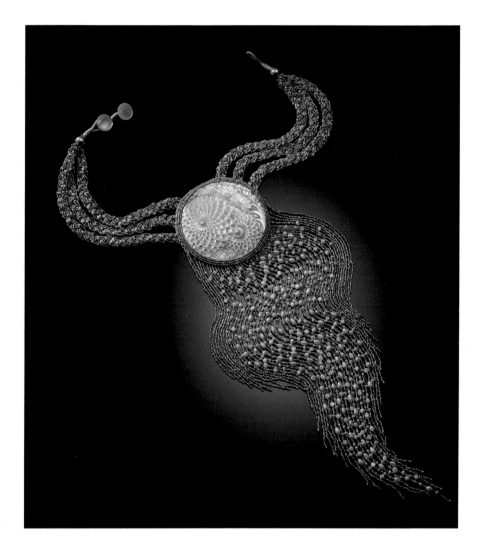

MARTIN DOUGLAS KILMER
Born 1945, Binghamton, New York
Resides in Petaluma, California

Chrysanthemums Weeping Dew on a Moonlit Summer Night. 1989. Necklace of strung and braided glass and antique cut-metal seed beads, with a mother-of-pearl centerpiece on leather, surrounded by bead embroidery and a fall of seed beads with rice pearls, finished with a wrapped loop-and-button closure, 18 × 4 × ½". Collection Obi-ko, San Francisco, California

Kilmer says this piece, like most of his work, emerged from years of collecting beads and other wonderful objects. When he acquired the mother-of-pearl chrysanthemum, it adorned the lid of an ordinary face-powder compact. The chrysanthemum was the perfect companion piece to his collection of pearls, antique French cut-steel beads, and glass seed beads. The artist feels that this is one of those rare pieces whose elements work so well together that he has no desire to make any changes.

Rainfall on a Clear and Sunny Day. 1990. Choker of hammered and hand-wrought sterling silver, with some segments wrapped in strung turquoise and metal seed beads, and with a tassel of turquoise and metal seed beads, 15 × 5 × ½". Collection the artist

See also COLLABORATION

DAN KING-LEHMAN
Born 1947, Fresno, California

EVE KING-LEHMAN
Born 1952, Bethesda, Maryland
Reside in Topanga, California

Ace. 1987. Sculpture of found tennis racket restrung with beaded wire and covered with strung seed beads; and metal bar holding nineteen Styrofoam balls wrapped with wire-strung seed beads and finished with wired, beaded "sprigs," 24 × 52 × 12". Collection First Interstate Bank of California, San Francisco

The King-Lehmans' art is collaborative, the result of two artistic minds working in unison. They think big, wanting to extend the established boundaries of beadwork and to create sculpture of a size more readily associated with the traditional mediums of metal, stone, and assemblage.

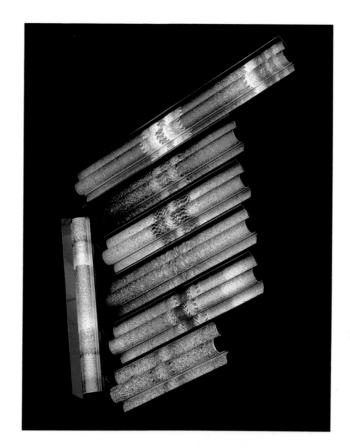

Wing. 1991. Sculpture of wire-strung seed beads wrapped around functioning fluorescent lights, each with mirrored reflectors, $40 \times 36 \times 5''$. Collection the artists

JOANNE A. LAESSIG
Born 1955, Cleveland Heights, Ohio
Resides in Cleveland Heights, Ohio

The Week I Didn't Go to Ireland. 1987. Wall panel embroidered with transparent seed beads sewn over silver lamé, with pearl beads and goldstone fragments, mounted on plywood, $9 \times 12 \times \frac{1}{2}''$. Collection Joanne Bast, Littlestown, Pennsylvania

An enamelist, Laessig was first attracted to glass beads because with them she could achieve many of the same color and light effects as with enamel, but with a more direct physical involvement. Bead embroidery also allowed her to introduce the element of line and linear repetition, significant components in her imagery.

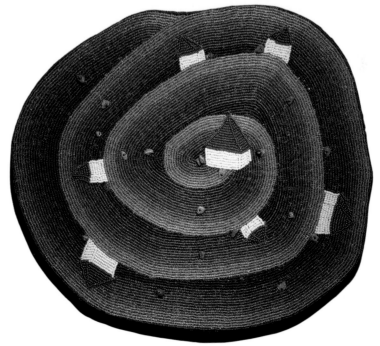

Jeanne Leffingwell
Born 1954, Denver, Colorado
Resides in Moscow, Idaho

OPPOSITE

Sky Curtain. 1985. Architectural sculpture of glass seed beads strung on polyester multifilament thread, mounted on steel-rod supports, with nickel-plated copper-tubing rod covers, c. 30 × 30 × 30'. Collection City of Anchorage, installed in the atrium of the William A. Egan Civic and Convention Center, Anchorage, Alaska

Leffingwell doesn't hesitate to think big, and the statistics of this artwork stagger the imagination. *Sky Curtain* has more than five million beads strung in twenty-three hundred strands on more than six miles of polyester thread. The sculpture weighs about two hundred pounds and took almost seven thousand hours to complete. The artist·employed five assistants to string the beads from color charts she designed by computer. Leffingwell, who once lived in Alaska, was inspired to create this piece by the northern lights, and chose the medium of transparent-glass seed and bugle beads for two reasons: they reflect and transmit light, and they are an art form familiar to the Native American women of Alaska. The sculpture is a site-specific commission for a public atrium; Leffingwell liked the feminine quality of the building's curving lines and believed that the shape of the sculpture should reflect them.

Coriolis. 1987. Architectural sculpture of seed and bugle beads strung on multifilament polyester thread, mounted on an armature of chrome-plated steel, 11 × 10' diameter. Collection City of Anchorage, installed in the Ship Creek Water Treatment Facility, Anchorage, Alaska

Since this sculpture was designed to hang in a public water-treatment building, Leffingwell spent time looking at water and thinking about it. Ultimately she was inspired while watching water swirl down the bathtub's drain at the end of her bath. She spent two weeks "filling gallon jugs, spinning them around, and watching the water drain out." The Coriolis force for which the sculpture is named is the swirling motion of a moving body caused by the inertia of that body in relation to the rotational field of the earth; in the Northern Hemisphere the motion is counterclockwise; in the Southern Hemisphere it is clockwise.

RICHARD LeMIEUX
Born 1955, Muskegon, Michigan
Resides in Thessaloniki, Greece

Tucson. 1981. Seed beads stitched to stretched and painted canvas, $14 \times 14 \times \frac{1}{4}$". Collection the artist

As LeMieux notes, "A great deal of energy goes into beading because of the nature of the material. Therefore, a relatively small beaded image can have the same 'presence' as a large painting." LeMieux completed this piece shortly after moving to Europe. The image relates to "the positive aspects of being in a place that is alien to one's nature." Despite its title, this work is not so much about Tucson, Arizona, as a geographical location as it is about a series of ideas that originated there.

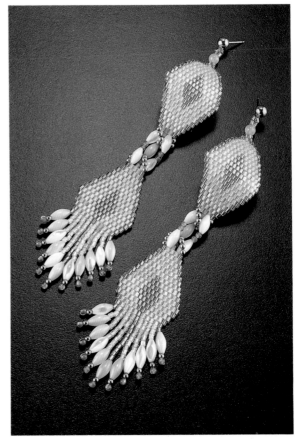

GWYN LEWIS
Born 1962, San Francisco, California
Resides in Oakley, California

Seafoam. 1988. Earrings in brick stitch, with top section shaped by a thread stretched between the top and bottom points, each $5\frac{1}{2} \times 1\frac{1}{2}$". Collection the artist

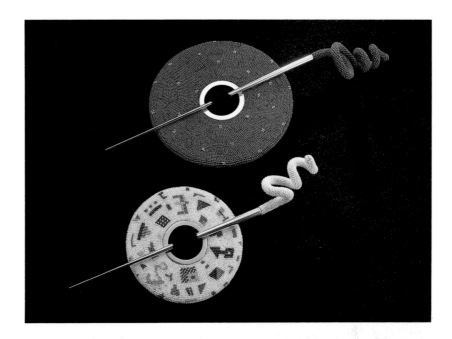

Jacqueline Lillie

Born 1941, Marseilles, France
Resides in Vienna, Austria

Fibulas. 1990. Disks of beaded textile in a knotting technique, with silver frame; stickpins of silver and beaded textile over wire; large fibula, 3¾″ diameter, stickpin, 7¾ × ¼″; small fibula, 2¾″ diameter, stickpin, 6½ × ¼″. Courtesy Rosanne Raab Associates, collection the artist

Lillie is attracted to the simplicity of basic geometric shapes. She feels that "a piece of jewelry is not only a reflection of one's personality, but also an expression of the age in which one lives. Contemporary jewelry must be more incisive and multipurpose than hitherto."

Necklace. 1985. Beaded shapes knotted over silver spheres fabricated by the artist, 1 × 32″. Courtesy Rosanne Raab Associates, collection the artist

This is one of Lillie's earlier pieces. Its style leans toward that of the Wiener Werkstätte, a design movement stemming from a period of artistic, scientific, and philosophical ferment in Vienna early in this century, as the artist notes. Although this style served as her initial source of inspiration, Lillie has since been drawn to a broad spectrum of influences: African and Native American jewelry, Russian Constructivism, Art Deco design, the Bauhaus. Her intention, she says, "is not that of a revivalist, but to produce work that reflects attention to minute detail and a subtle use of color."

JACQUELINE LILLIE

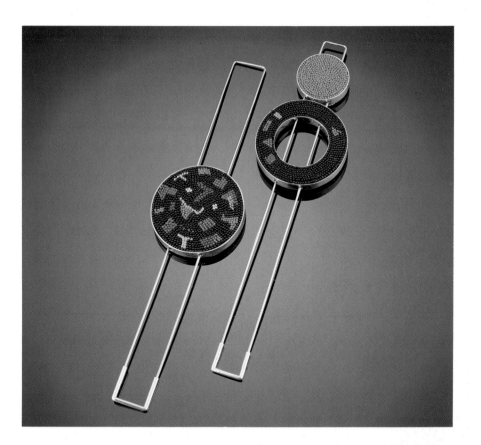

OPPOSITE:

Necklace and brooch. 1990. Necklace of graduated spheres covered with knotted-bead textile, with silver inserts and clasp; brooch of knotted-bead textile mounted in silver frame; necklace, 1¼ × 23"; brooch, 1½". Courtesy Rosanne Raab Associates, collection the artist

Lillie's jewelry reflects her concern with quality in design and precision in execution. She secures the finest and smallest beads she can find between tiny knots of silk thread to form a textile with a high degree of flexibility and suppleness. Lillie brings the same consideration of quality and design to the hand fabrication of her silver spheres and findings, integral to the overall composition of each piece. While she is attentive to the trends of fashion, she designs her jewelry so that it is timeless and may be "adjusted to the mood and wishes of the wearer."

ABOVE RIGHT:

Pendulum brooches. 1990. Silver with knotted-bead inserts and steel pin, each 8 × 1½". Courtesy Rosanne Raab Associates, collection the artist

RIGHT:

Ear studs. 1990. Two pairs of earrings of knotted-bead textile set in silver frames, disks, each 1¾" diameter; squares, each 1 × 1". Courtesy Rosanne Raab Associates, collection the artist

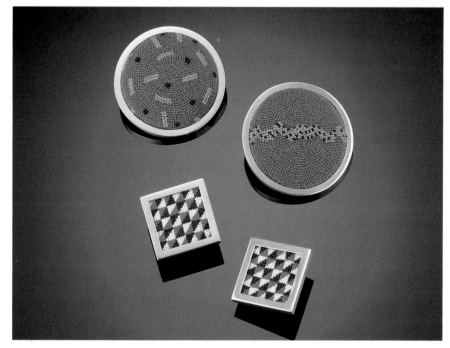

MERRY MAKELA
Born 1947, Little Rock, Arkansas
Resides in College Station, Texas

Necklace. 1989. Circular netting with seed beads and opal chips, $20 \times \frac{1}{2}''$. Collection Center for the Study of Beadwork, Portland, Oregon

MARGOT MARCOTTE
Born 1969, Munich, Germany
Resides in Ithaca, New York

Power Vision Shirt. 1989. Shirt woven in one piece, on a large hand-built loom, of size 10° seed beads, folded and sewn down the sides, with the threads in the neck opening cut and woven back into the garment, $14 \times 17''$. Collection the artist

SHERRY MARKOVITZ
Born 1947, Chicago, Illinois
Resides in Seattle, Washington

Sea Bear. 1990. Sculpture of mixed mediums on a papier-mâché base formed over a taxidermy mold, painted with acrylics, and covered with strung seed beads glued to the surface, with shells, branches, and glass eyes, $18 \times 25 \times 29''$. Collection Seattle Art Museum, Washington, 33.3% Fractional Interest Gift of Terry Hunziker

Although Markovitz did no beadwork as a child, she loved beads. In the fourth grade she drew images of Navajo beadwork. As an adult, this early fascination with beads and their surfaces led her to explore the possibilities of transformation through ornamentation and encrustation. In this piece she remembers walks on wonderful beaches in Florida and Washington State. Capturing the qualities of light on sand in the bear's beaded coat, the work expresses the fertility of creative thought that comes from roaming free.

SHERRY MARKOVITZ

OPPOSITE:

Jake's Stag. 1990. Sculpture of mixed mediums on a papier-mâché base formed from a taxidermy mold, painted with acrylics, and covered with strung and glued seed beads, with antlers, shells, fur, and glass eyes, 53 × 62 × 38". Collection Jake Millett, Seattle

Markovitz created this work for her son, Jake. Blue, the color of the sky, water, and clarity, unifies Markovitz's diverse themes. This animal-head trophy, one of a series made from casts of dead animals, speaks of metamorphosis, of life beyond death. Markovitz's sculptures embody the wild, natural environment of the Pacific Northwest, where she makes her home.

NOME MAY

Born 1966, Sydney, Australia
Resides in Taos, New Mexico

Magic. 1989. Wand of bamboo shaft covered with size 13° charlotte beads in peyote stitch (Native American variation), with quartz-crystal tip and fringe terminating in gemstone beads, 8½ × ¾" diameter. Collection the artist

LINDA MCCORMICK

Born 1949, Knoxville, Iowa
Resides in Indianola, Iowa

Skywards. 1990. Crocheted-beadwork miniature wheelchair with wings of wire wrapped in silk thread and incorporating feathers and additional beads, 13¾ × 10 × 4". Collection the artist

When McCormick was paralyzed in an automobile accident in 1976, she had long been using fiber and beads as a medium. She began a series of works on the winged-wheelchair theme in order to transcend the effects of her injury and hopes that they "may help people to look upon the wheelchair in a positive light, with a renewed sense of respect for its dignity."

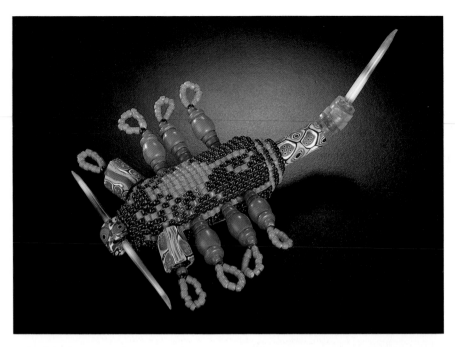

LUISA MORCA-BUSH
Born 1957, Los Angeles, California
Resides in Bellingham, Washington

Stinger. 1989. Sculpture of seed beads in square stitch, with antique trade beads and African porcupine quills, $6 \times 4 \times 2''$. Collection the artist

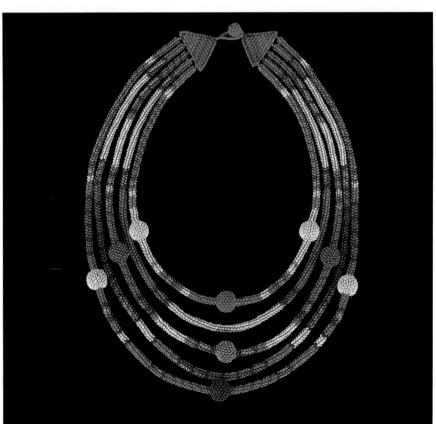

KATHLYN MOSS
Born 1944, Oakland, California
Resides in Corvallis, Oregon

Planets. 1991. Necklace of peyote-stitched tubes and balls with square-stitched tabs on leather, $12 \times 7 \times \frac{1}{2}''$. Collection the artist

CHERI MOSSIE
Born 1956, Kansas City, Missouri
Resides in Oracle, Arizona

Imagine. 1981. Belt buckle of seed beads embroidered on leather over metal, 2½ × 3½". Collection John Bill Williams, Tucson, Arizona

Mossie takes a spiritual approach to her work, finding, through prayer and dreams, just the right design for the person who has commissioned a beadwork piece from her. She notes that each finished work always has a special resonance for the intended recipient.

Ye Are Gods. 1989. Belt buckle of seed beads embroidered on leather over metal, 3½ × 4½". Collection Ray Gonzales, San Manuel, Arizona

The owner of this buckle is a rancher. When she began it, Mossie had a dream that *Ye Are Gods* should tell a creation story, so she made an image with a vivid allegory. The little ant man is a symbol of perseverance and physical force. Above his head is a scatter of gold beads, representing the magic of the god force, which he may use as he chooses. He has created a bubble within which he lives and grows; this is the universe as he knows it. He shares this world with a butterfly, a symbol of transformation and possibility. Meanwhile, his foot is anchored at the edge of the bubble, in contact with the god force outside, the source of his life's inspiration.

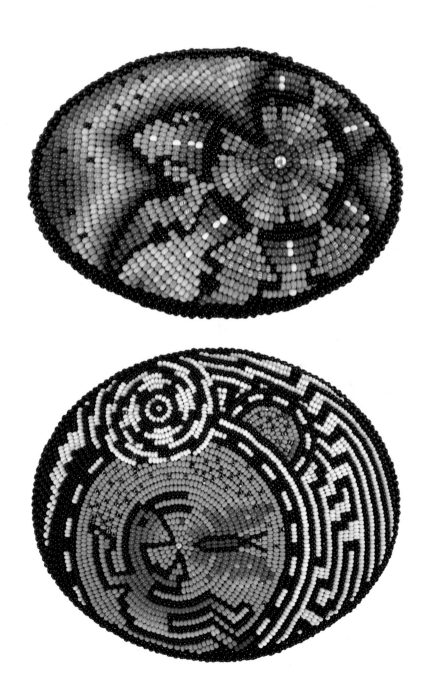

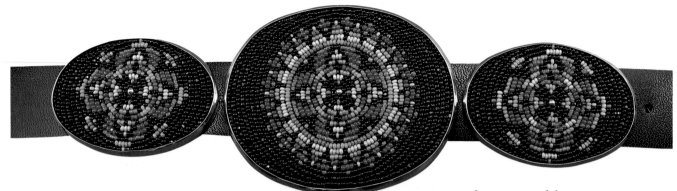

JUANITA NELSON
Born 1956, Denver, Colorado
Resides in Bayfield, Colorado

___

Black Conchos. 1988. Belt of bead embroidery on leather, mounted in handmade silver conchos on a leather strip, $2\frac{1}{4} \times 30 \times \frac{1}{4}$". Collection Françoise, Taos, New Mexico

HOWARD NEWCOMB
Born 1947, Santa Monica, California
Resides in Portland, Oregon

___

Blue and White Comets. 1989. Ten-strand choker of porcelain beads in twenty shades, made by the artist, with handmade sterling-silver clasp, 16×1". Collection the artist

GRETCHEN NEWMARK
Born 1949, Oakland, California
Resides in Portland, Oregon

TOP: *Snake*. 1989. Wand of beadwork in peyote stitch over a stick of wood, 18 × ½" diameter. BOTTOM: *Frog and Lotus*. 1988. Rattle of a gourd topped with flamingo and hen feathers, handle covered with seed beads in peyote stitch, 18 × 2½" diameter. Both pieces collection the artist

Newmark finds inspiration in ethnic and folk art and likes to retain the naive qualities of direct design and bright color in her work. The simple rattles a friend makes from found objects such as palm fronds motivated her to create her own. Her rattle is made from a dried gourd she has decorated with hen and flamingo feathers from a neighbor's aviary. The images of the frog and lotus have special meaning for the artist, the frog in particular being her personal fetish.

To create the snake, Newmark spent several months searching for a stick whose form expresses the intrinsic personality of a snake. She beaded the stick in segments, with different designs in each, to avoid repeating the same pattern over and over. These variations in patterns, and the use of complementary colors, create a rich visual impression. Newmark left part of the stick unbeaded to celebrate the snake's sticklike nature.

LINDSAY OBERMEYER
Born 1966, Saint Louis, Missouri
Resides in Chicago, Illinois

This Side of Paradise. 1988. Wallpiece of free embroidery on damask with plastic, stone, and glass seed beads and buttons, 11½ × 13½ × ½". Collection the artist

Garden of the Soul. 1988. Wallpiece of free embroidery on commercial fabric with plastic, stone, and glass seed beads and buttons, 15 × 14 × ½". Collection the artist

CONSTANCE O'SHAUGHNESSY
Born 1940, Plymouth, Indiana
Resides in Alexandria, Virginia

Beaded jasper pin. 1989. Pin constructed of glass seed beads and gemstone beads strung on nylon monofilament and woven through a metal backing, 3 × 2 × 1¼". Collection Diana Barhyte, Alexandria, Virginia

CAROL PERRENOUD
Born 1957, Los Angeles, California
Resides in Wilsonville, Oregon

Beaded Victorian miser purse. 1989. Crocheted purse of cotton thread, nylon blending filament, and seed beads; fringe with bugle and seed beads, including size 13° three-cut beads, 11 × 2½ × ¼". Collection the artist

Perrenoud re-creates Victorian and turn-of-the-century clothing. This purse was inspired by Edwardian finger purses usually carried by men, but Perrenoud's version is so frilly and pink it seems the embodiment of Victorian femininity. Unlike this one, the early purses had little or no fringe. "The most interesting feature is how the purse opens," the artist notes. "The handle threads go through the front flap and connect to the top front of the bag. When the flap is opened, the threads are pulled apart so that one can get inside, which makes for a secure pouch."

DONALD PIERCE
Born 1935, Fossil, Oregon
Resides in Coos Bay, Oregon, and
Fort Saint James, British Columbia

OPPOSITE LEFT:

Art Deco. 1989. Necklace loom-woven of size 14° three-cut seed beads, with padded center, 10¾ × 5½". Collection the artist

OPPOSITE RIGHT:

Shimmy and Shake. 1989. Necklace loom-woven with rolled-copper bugle beads prestrung on the warp and three-cut beads woven in, 19 × 6". Collection the artist

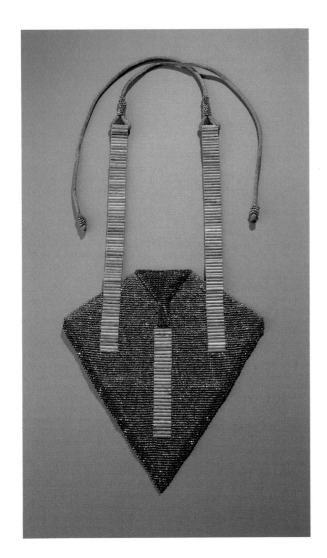

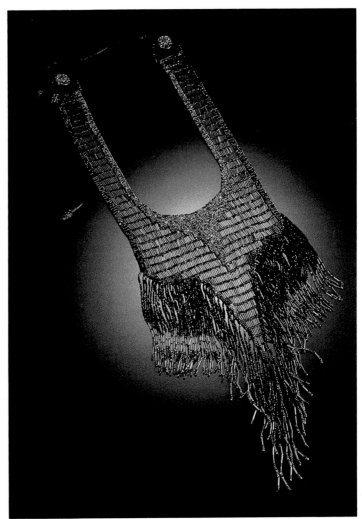

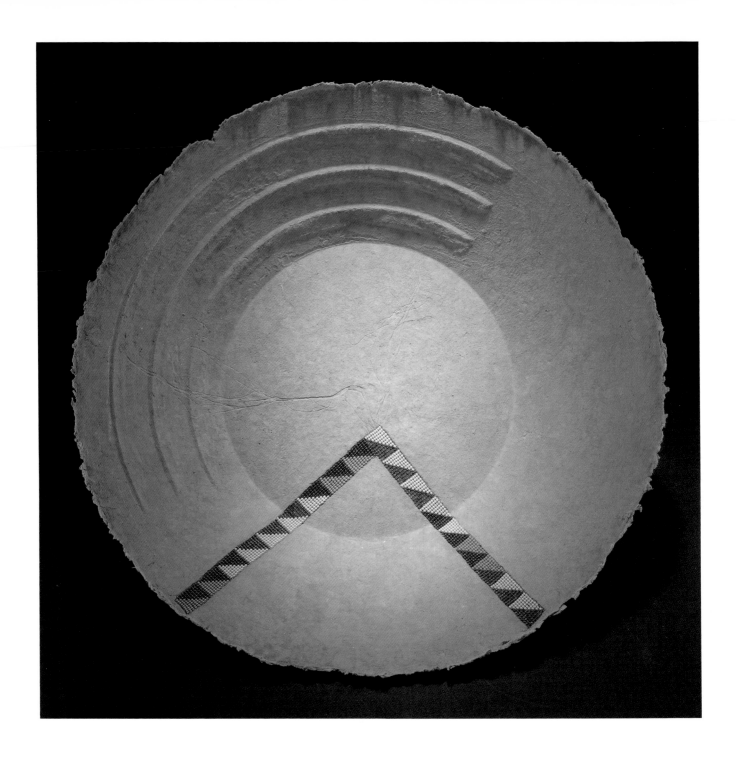

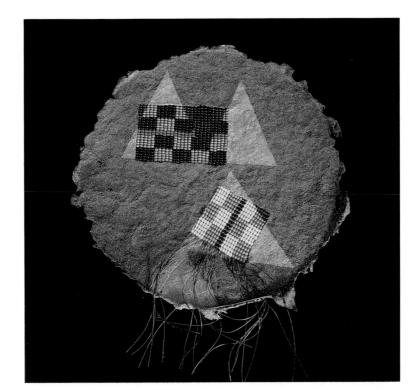

SUSAN PLANALP

Born 1946, Saint Joseph, Missouri
Resides in Boulder, Colorado

OPPOSITE:

Island Bowl. 1990. Vessel of mold-formed, handmade paper with embedded loom-woven seed-bead strips, 5 × 14" diameter. Collection the artist

Planalp sees her work as an amalgam of the visual and the tactile. She uses beads in her paper pieces because she likes the comforting predictability of their orderly rows in contrast to the sloppiness of casting paper. She embeds the bead strips in such a way that they seem to grow from within the paper ground. Planalp relates that artifacts seen in the Anasazi Museum in Mesa Verde, Arizona, and Amish quilts have had a profound effect on the colors and materials she uses in her work.

Secrets. 1990. Wallpiece of mold-formed, handmade, painted paper with embedded loom-woven seed-bead strips and thread, ½ × 6" diameter. Collection Center for the Study of Beadwork, Portland, Oregon

Night Dancers. 1990. Wallpiece of mold-formed, handmade, painted paper, with embedded loom-woven seed-bead strips and thread, ½ × 6" diameter. Collection Center for the Study of Beadwork, Portland, Oregon

Sylvia Pomeroy

Born 1962, Berkeley, California
Resides in Fortine, Montana

Frogs' OXO Tic-Tac-Toe Game Set. 1990.
Game board of loom-woven beadwork, finished with a handspun and -knitted silk tape, with eleven peyote-stitch frog game pieces (seven pictured), including a referee frog, each $2 \times 2 \times 2$"; game board, 7×7". Collection the artist

In early 1988 Pomeroy began making peyote-stitch frogs, lizards, salamanders, and iguanas to amuse herself and as a break from the knitting and spinning from which she makes her living. After receiving an enthusiastic response to her "critters," she became intrigued with the idea of combining several with a game board. She considered making a chess set, but settled on tic-tac-toe, a game of yes, no, and maybe, a paradigm of life.

Pat Poole
Born 1953, Memphis, Tennessee
Resides in Greeneville, Tennessee

Tree of Life. 1989. Window or wall hanging, woven in peyote stitch with three-cut seed beads, fringe composed of long bugle beads and other glass beads, design developed by Andrew Frank, 21 × 9". Collection the artist

Triple Spiral. 1988. Brooch or barrette woven in peyote stitch with three-cut seed beads, fringe composed of seed beads, rice pearls, and other glass beads, with a natural-crystal pendant, design developed by Andrew Frank, 5 × 3½ × ¼". Collection the artist

BARBARA JEANNE RICE
Born 1934, Wenatchee, Washington
Resides in Colfax, Washington

Occasional Flights: Lilium Caelestis Rosa. 1986. Basket of acrylic and cotton yarns in Peruvian coiling stitch, with twined half-turns and beaded overlay, 3½ × 4½″ diameter. Collection the artist

HELEN ROGERS
Born 1954, Atlanta, Georgia
Resides in Davis, California

Earrings. 1986. Brick stitch with looped fringe, each 2¾ × ¾″. Collection the artist

Cat Mummy. 1990. Sculpture of fabric and wood dowels, covered with heavy canvas embroidered with seed beads, with raw linen on the foot portion, $24\frac{1}{2} \times 7 \times 4''$. Collection the artist

Rogers does not recall the origin of the idea for this piece, but she remembers pondering it for a couple of years. The artist first saw an image of an Egyptian cat mummy in the studio of a fellow painter who shares her love for cats. The idea of the cat as an object of reverence and a bringer of good luck was the inspiration for this work. After she had begun to cover the body of the piece with beads, Rogers discovered that the ancient Egyptians had covered some human mummies with nets of beadwork. She was pleased by the coincidence.

Equally intriguing to her are carved Yoruba twin figures, or *ibeji.* These sculptures are clothed in heavily beaded garments. Like the cat mummies, they are symbols of reverence and good fortune. Rogers has come to see her sculpture as a merging of the imagery of the Egyptian cat mummy and the Yoruba *ibeji.* In a museum she once saw a mummy of two animals wrapped as a single unit, which bore a striking resemblance to a Yoruba twin figure. Her sculpture is somewhat larger than actual cat mummies, which are bound in thin strips of linen of varying shades of tan. The crossing of the fabric strips forms a pattern much like that of a log-cabin quilt. In designing the beaded body, Rogers wanted to capture this pattern and to accentuate the image of wrapping, like a baby's bunting.

AXEL RUSSMEYER
Born 1964, Bad Oldesole, Germany
Resides in Hamburg, Germany

Wooden Box for Seven Spheres. 1989.
Sculpture of antique peyote-stitched metal
seed beads over larger wood beads, with a
turned, segmented grenadill-wood container
designed by the artist and made by Harald
Mueller, spheres, ½ to ¾" diameter, average;
container, 5¾ × 1". Collection the artist

Russmeyer uses the beaded sphere and tube
as the basic components of his sculptural
jewelry. The simplicity of these forms enhances the intrinsic beauty and classic shape
of the tiny beads from which his ornaments
are composed. They have the strength of
larger-scale works despite their diminutive
size. These spheres are also beads, meant to
be worn on a leather thong or gold chain.

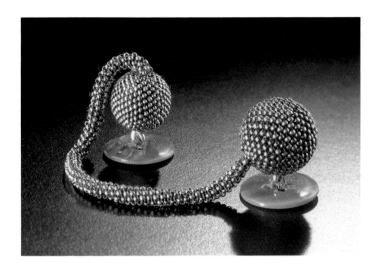

Decoration for Two Buttonholes. 1989. Sculpture of seed beads peyote-stitched over two wood beads, each sphere fastened to a mother-of-pearl button and connected by a peyote-stitched beaded tube, $\frac{1}{2} \times 2 \times \frac{1}{2}$". Collection the artist

PAM SAPORTA
Born 1955, New York City
Resides in Pike, California

Beads. 1989–90. Group of beaded beads in peyote stitch over wood, largest bead $1\frac{3}{4} \times 1$" diameter; smallest bead $\frac{1}{2} \times \frac{1}{4}$" diameter. Collection the artist and Center for the Study of Beadwork, Portland, Oregon

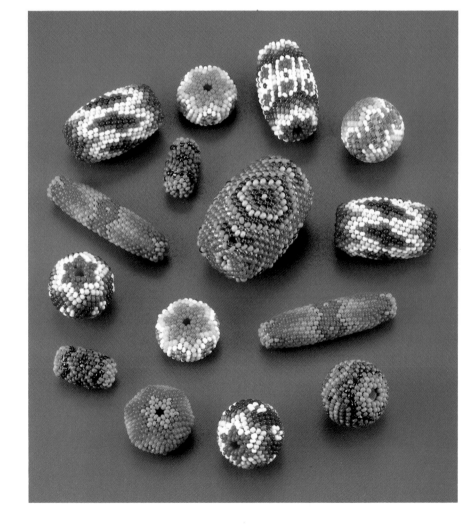

SKIP SCHUCKMANN
Born 1945, Denver, Colorado
Resides in Ojai, California

Annie's Magpie Necklace. 1976–77. T-necklace peyote-stitched in size 11° to 13° seed beads, mounted on brain-tanned muledeer-skin neckband, neckband, 2 × 16"; pectoral, 14 × 7". Collection Annie Buckley, Denver, Colorado

In this elegant necklace, Schuckmann approaches beadwork with serious artistic and spiritual intent. He has created specific, earthy images, using the design elements of color and form to explore the geometric cosmology of the number seven. His piece follows a seven-part schema: (1) energy as sky, (2) earth as mass, (3) fire and water as the center and as creation and annihilation, (4) North as wisdom, (5) South as innocence, (6) West as intuition, (7) East as intelligence. The necklace is composed of seven sections and, with its focus on spiritual matters, typifies much early hippie beadwork; it was created for a wedding. Objects of this quality inspired many others, and have helped rekindle interest in beadwork as a vehicle for artistic expression.

Bottle. 1978. Vessel covered in peyote-stitched (Native American variation) seed beads, with lid of carved copal amber, inlaid glass gem, and leather base, 4¼ × 2¼" diameter. Collection Elsiejane Schuckmann, Elko, Nevada

JOYCE J. SCOTT
Born 1948, Baltimore, Maryland
Resides in Baltimore, Maryland

What You Mean, Jungle Music. 1989.
Neckpiece of glass, metal, and plastic beads,
thread, photographs, plastic, wire, and
diffraction-grading plastic, $17 \times 12 \times 2\frac{1}{2}''$.
Collection Jenette Kahn, New York City

Scott creates wearable sculpture with glass
beads because she has an affection for their
brilliant translucency and opacity. She believes this radiance activates her work in a
special way. Scott's work, incorporating
brightly colored, seemingly humorous figures, invites the viewer to touch, observe,
and learn. She created this piece after hearing
rap music, dejuiced for a mass audience, used
in an advertising jingle for a soft drink.
While this piece is about that particular
event, it is also, more generally, about the
insensitivity with which white culture co-
opts African-American music for its own
purposes, while turning a blind eye to the
music's origins.

Headdress. 1987. Hat of free-form peyote
stitch, with various glass beads, $5 \times 7''$ diameter. Collection the artist

JOYCE J. SCOTT

The Sneek. 1990. Sculptural neckpiece of
two-drop peyote stitch, c. $20 \times 9 \times 9''$. Collection the artist

Here Scott's subject is urban violence, the
assault on and murder of a woman. The
victim lies sprawled in the foreground, while
her attacker, at left, tries to flee the scene. The
large yellow face represents society's horror
and revulsion at the crime, while the figures
behind the face, chasing and grabbing the
murderer, depict revenge. The harsh, brilliant
colors embody the sharpness of emotions created by such a crime.

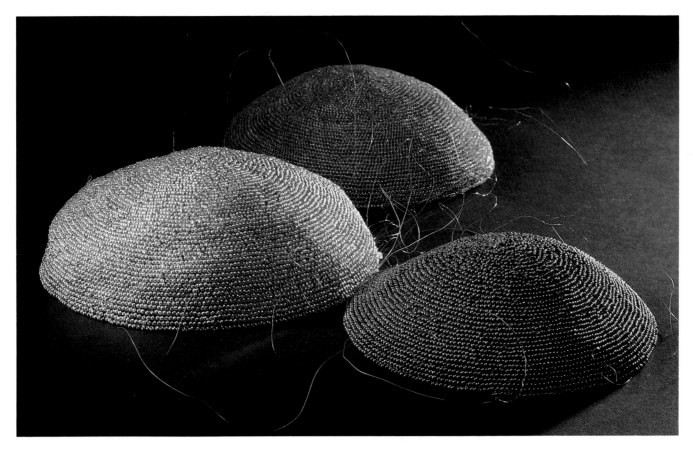

VERENA SIEBER-FUCHS
Born 1943, Appenzell, Switzerland
Resides in Zurich, Switzerland

Untitled. 1982. Sculpture of crocheted silk with metal seed beads, each element $6\frac{1}{4} \times 6\frac{1}{4} \times 1\frac{1}{2}''$. Collection the artist

Armband. 1978. Ornament of crocheted silk and metal seed beads, $6 \times 6 \times 2\frac{3}{4}''$. Collection the artist

Sieber-Fuchs's beadwork is sculptural: form as fabricated through the incremental elaboration of texture; she coils and twists her pieces into unconventional shapes. Light playing on the pebbled contours of beaded surfaces enhances the sometimes gossamer, sometimes dense substructure of filament.

MARCIE STONE
Born 1951, New York City
Resides in San Diego, California

Basket. 1990. Vessel coiled from pine needles and silk thread with surface embellishment of malachite, amethyst, and flat
peyote-stitched seed-bead forms, 3½ × 4½"
diameter. Collection the artist

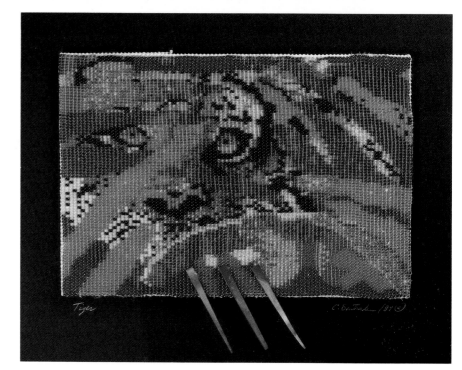

CID SUNTRADER
Born 1948, New Orleans, Louisiana
Resides in Sacramento, California

Hiding from Tiger. 1989. Wallpiece of
stitched seed-bead tapestry on needlepoint
canvas, 5 × 7½". Private collection

NATALIE TATZ
Born 1951, Sheboygan, Wisconsin
Resides in Santa Fe, New Mexico

Winter Ice. 1989. Brooch and earrings appliquéd with antique glass and metal seed beads and various kinds of pearls, backed with silk, brooch, 3½ × 2″; earrings, each 2¾ × 1¾″. Collection the artist

Tapestry Jar. 1988. Walnut jar with lid covered in size 18° glass and metal seed beads in peyote stitch, 2¾ × 1½″ diameter. Collection the artist

86 Tisa

KEN TISA

Born 1945, Philadelphia, Pennsylvania
Resides in New York City

OPPOSITE:

The Secret of Al Tarxien. 1990. Wallpiece
of glass seed and bugle beads, sequins, pearl
buttons, and cowrie shells, embroidered on
cotton canvas, 34 × 31". Collection the artist

Tisa is intrigued by the symbols of ancient
myths and spiritual secrets, especially as portrayed in the Brazilian and Caribbean celebrations of Carnival. After seeing an
exhibition of Haitian beaded and sequined
banners while in graduate school, he was
compelled to change the direction of his work
and chose to travel the world, studying tribal
cultures. This piece combines three elements
Tisa employs in much of his work: the human form, the snake or spiral image, and a
central abstract shape, which in this work is
based on the silhouette of the ancient Mal-
tese temple Al Tarxien. Here, the artist says,
the labyrinth created by the snakes "represents the realm of immortality reached by a
real or symbolic death and rebirth on another
plane."

CAMILLA TRONDSEN

Born 1950, Portland, Oregon
Resides in Portland, Oregon

RIGHT:

Lobsters and ***Peruvian Birds***. 1990. Earrings loom-woven of square, two-cut seed
beads, each 1½ × 1½". Collection the artist

ELIZABETH TUTTLE

Born 1946, Minneapolis, Minnesota
Resides in Madison, Wisconsin

BELOW:

Jeweled Wall. 1984. Wallpiece crocheted of
multiple strands of cotton thread, with transparent seed beads embroidered over the entire surface, 8 × 12". Collection the artist

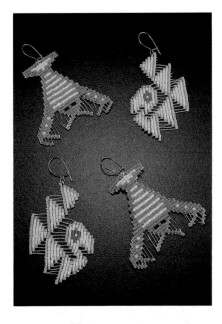

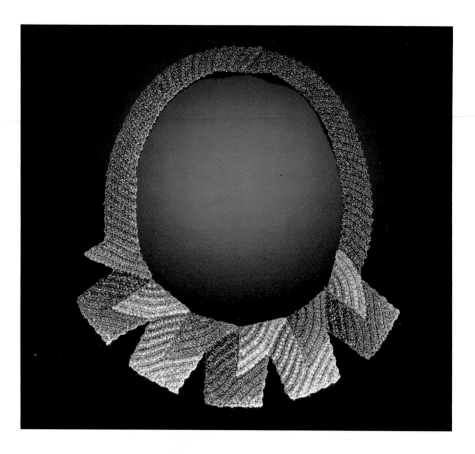

ELIZABETH TUTTLE

Shadow Collar. 1985. Collar crocheted of multiple strands of cotton sewing thread, with transparent seed beads embroidered over the entire surface, 11″ × 9″. Collection Mary Ann Gerlach, Elm Grove, Wisconsin

SETSU UENO
Born 1929, Troutdale, Oregon
Resides in Portland, Oregon

Miniature hats. 1990. Group of tiny hats hand-sewn with size 14° to 22° seed beads, on porcelain heads, average hat size ½ × 1 × ½″. Collection the artist

Ueno once wove large wall hangings; now she has progressed downward in scale to the intriguing possibilities of miniatures. She works under a lighted magnifying glass, using surgical tweezers to assemble her minute beaded hats, ring by tiny ring.

GLADYS URSCHEL
Born 1913, Michigan City, Indiana
Resides in Valparaiso, Indiana

Butterflies. 1985–86. Wall hanging of joined loom-woven strips, 26½ × 24½". Collection the artist

After several years of knitting, needlepoint, and crewel embroidery, Urschel wanted to work in a new medium. On a trip to Chicago she saw beaded-wire flowers and was fired to create her own. The idea for larger weavings grew slowly, but eventually she wanted a more demanding format than the necklaces she had been creating. Her husband, an engineer, designed a loom suitable for large weavings. With this loom and specially designed graph paper, she set about weaving a bead tapestry for each member of her family. Her first wall hanging was based on Native American motifs. In creating this work, she realized that her designs need not be limited to Native traditions, and she turned her attention to other kinds of patterns, especially those of the Middle East. The poetry of Omar Khayyam has been a particular source of inspiration. Whatever the source, all of Urschel's bead tapestries are characterized by floral motifs arranged in a formal symmetry.

DONNA WASSERSTROM
Born 1944, Cleveland, Ohio
Resides in Columbus, Ohio

Zachor (Remember). 1988. Tallith bag of suede and silk, with seed-bead appliqué on the front, 8 × 11½ × 1½". Collection the artist

Wasserstrom created this liturgical piece for her husband. The tallith is a prayer shawl worn by observant Jews during the celebration of Shabbat and the high holidays, Rosh Hashanah and Yom Kippur, and by tradition passed from father to son. Wasserstrom expresses her feelings about the Holocaust in imagery and symbols derived from Jewish life and history, with an emphasis on *zachor*, remembrance. These symbols carry multiple meanings, some contradictory; among them is the shofar, the trumpet sounded in the joyful ceremony of the new year, but also used as an alarm. Within the Star of David at center is the Hebrew letter *zachor*, which symbolizes the need for Jews to remember the lives lost in the fight to practice faith freely. The style and colors were influenced by the work of Marc Chagall.

BETSEY-ROSE WEISS
Born 1955, Evanston, Illinois
Resides in Morehead City, North Carolina

Night Blooms. 1989. Necklace of seed beads embroidered on felt, glued to leather, and trimmed with sewn beadwork, 3½ × 5½". Collection the artist

STEVE WOFFORD
Born 1953, Denver, Colorado
Resides in Yelm, Washington

Miniature vessels. 1987–89. Coiled baskets beaded with size 16° and 18° beads, largest basket, 1″ diameter. Collections the artist, family, and friends

Influenced by his Native American roots and using beading techniques learned from his mother, Wofford creates works that elaborate on traditional forms while giving them a modern sensibility.

NATACHA WOLTERS
Born 1938, Paris, France
Resides in Berlin, Germany

Autumn. 1989. Neckpiece knitted in silk in the artist's own technique, in which the neckpiece is beaded on both sides, using size 17° to 20° glass and metal seed beads, with gilded-silver clasp fabricated by Alfred Schmiedl, 9½ × 8¾″. Collection the artist

Connie Wyatt
Born 1949, Birmingham, Alabama
Resides in Alexandria, Virginia

Winter Dreams: A Trilogy. 1989. Screen of loom-woven beadwork with netting and surface embellishment, mounted in wood frame, 15 × 33 × 1″. Collection the artist

Appendix A
The Manufacture of Seed Beads

The craft of glass seed-bead manufacture is very old. Evidence exists that the ancient Egyptians produced a small quantity of microbeads by bending a molten-glass sheet around a wire to form a tube, which was then cut laterally into small pieces. Small beads resulted when the pieces were reheated until the sharp edges had grown round and smooth.

In the first century B.C. glassworkers made an important breakthrough in producing seed beads when they developed the technology to draw long, slender tubes from molten glass. The invention of the blowpipe in Phoenicia at about this same time made production even easier. However, the oldest method of manufacturing drawn-glass beads without a blowpipe was developed by the bead makers of India two thousand years ago, and is still in use in that country today, as well as in Sri Lanka, Indonesia, and Malaysia.

Methods of Production

INDIA

The glassworkers of the village of Papanaidupet in southern India have a unique process for making drawn-glass seed beads, the *lada* method. According to Peter Francis, Jr., director of the Center for Bead Research in Lake Placid, New York, the glass master and his assistants first collect a hundred-pound ball of molten glass, called a gather, on the end of a long, wide metal tube, or *lada*. The assistants shape the gather into a cone by rolling it along a low wall. Once this is done, and while the glass is still plastic, a rod is forced through the *lada* to punch a hole through the glass. When the rod is removed, air flows through the *lada* into the glass and keeps the hole open. Then the whole affair is put back into the furnace to be reheated.

The *lada* extends beyond the back opening of the furnace so that air continues to enter the glass. The glass master then draws the glass, grasping the front end of the cone with a metal hook, and pulling. The first few pulls are not intact and are discarded. Once a good tube forms, the master draws the glass out continuously, hand over hand, walking back about fifteen feet from the furnace. He and two other glass-drawers take turns until all the glass has been drawn out. The whole process takes about five or six hours.

The manufacture of these slender glass tubes is the first step toward making seed beads. Once the tubes have cooled, they are cut into tiny segments, which are packed into a crucible with ash and stirred over heat for one-half hour, to smooth the sharp edges. The cooled bead-and-ash mixture is then put into a mortar and the ash is pounded out with a wood pestle, separating the finished beads, which are then strung into hanks.

EUROPE

In northern Italy, by the year A.D. 1480, drawn-glass microbeads were being produced. The bead maker began the process by gathering a pear-sized lump of molten glass on the end of a blowpipe. Next the worker blew a small puff of air into the gather, making a bubble. To get the bubble to stretch, he would gently swing the blowpipe like a pendulum. Once this step was executed, the hollow glass cylinder was returned to the furnace to be reheated until it was semifluid. In the next step, the drawing-out, the bead maker allowed one end of the cylinder to fall to the floor, then pulled away from it to create a long, slender glass tube.

While this single-person technique is still used, it is more usual in Europe for two artisans to work together. One glassworker collects the gather, blows in the air bubble, and reheats it. Once the hollow gather is plastic enough, an assistant attaches a metal rod, or punty, and walks quickly away, stretching out a very long tube. The resulting tube has thick and thin areas that will ultimately be beads of different sizes.

The next step is to break the tube into sections of about one yard in length. Bundles of these are then cut into bead-sized pieces by machines. After this, the raw beads are tumbled with hot sand (800–1000° F), until the rough edges are smooth. The hot sand-and-bead mixture cools as it tumbles, annealing the glass, so that the beads will not shatter. The mixture is then run through several sieves of various gauges, to remove the sand and sort the beads according to size.

The final step is the stringing of the beads into hanks. The author Virginia Osterland reports that workers accomplish this by holding a fan of several threaded seven-inch needles, which they scoop through a shallow, oblong bowl of beads. As the individual threads are filled with beads, they are set aside. Once all the threads are full, the lengths are evened out, so that each holds a similar number of beads. These threads are then tied into hanks, and are ready for market. Today, in France, Italy, and Czechoslovakia, this manufacturing process remains much the same, although machines are now used.

JAPAN

Beginning in the 1950s, the Japanese applied their technical expertise to the manufacture of seed beads. They have engineered the most advanced mechanical processes currently in use. Glass tubes are mechanically extruded from computer-controlled furnaces. This process creates beads of unusual consistency in size and shape. The Japanese have also developed new colors and finishes for their beads.

Bead Materials

While seed beads are traditionally of glass, they may be made from a variety of other materials, especially metals. Metal seed beads may be of steel, bronze, brass, or aluminum. These are manufactured in much the same way as their glass counterparts. As the tiny metal tube is extruded, it is drawn through a die to shape and texture it, so that each tiny bead may appear to be hand-faceted or wire-brushed. Few such beads have been pro-duced since World War II. Currently, aluminum predominates in the making of metal microbeads.

Bead Colors and Finishes
COLORS

Metallic oxides and salts are the basic ingredients for coloring glass. Some of these metallic agents, and the colors associated with them, are:

CADMIUM	Yellow, orange, red
CHROMIUM	Olive green, bright yellow
COBALT	Blue, dark blue, blue-violet
COPPER	Turquoise, red, ruby red, reddish brown
GOLD	Rose-pink, ruby red, garnet
IRON	Brown, green, yellow, black
MANGANESE	Pink, violet, clear, black
SELENIUM	Ruby red, true violet, clear
SILVER	Amber
TITANIUM	White

Some metals can create more than one color. These color differences are the result of controlled variations in the amount of metallic minerals used and of oxygen present in the furnace, as well as in the temperature during the heating or cooling of the glass. Black glass is made from a variety of colorants or techniques. For this reason, some "black" beads look dark purple or brown when held to the light.

While most coloring agents are common metals, such as iron and copper, some are rare and precious, such as cobalt and gold. The value of seed beads is determined not only by these colorants, but also by the era in which they were made. Beads manufactured before World War II, often by hand, with better materials, richer colors, and superior finishes, are the most valuable.

FINISHES

The glass used for making seed beads ranges in clarity from transparent to opaque, and is classed accordingly. Cathedral glass is completely transparent, with a saturated color and high light refraction. Opalescent glass is translucent, due to the addition of chemicals that give it a slightly clouded appearance. Greasy glass is somewhat more opaque, with a soft sheen that causes each bead to resemble a bit of colored Vaseline. Satin glass is slightly more opaque still, getting its tone-on-tone appearance from the way it is manufactured. There are two methods for producing this type of glass. In the first, air bubbles are stirred into the glass before it is formed into the gather. When the gather is drawn into a long tube, these bubbles also elongate, creating a striated effect, so that the glass resembles watered silk. In the second, glass strands are fused to the outside of the gather early in the beadmaking process. Again, as the gather is drawn out, these strands elongate and also create striations in the glass. Finally, opaque glass is solid in color and does not transmit light.

Another class of beads is manufactured in two or more layers. The white-heart bead is the most familiar of these. First, a gather of opaque glass, usually white, is formed into a hollow cylinder. Next, a layer of transparent glass in another color is applied over the opaque glass. The two colors are fused into a single cylinder, which is then drawn and finished in the usual way. This technique was developed to conserve the precious minerals used in the outer colors. Striped beads are made in a similar fashion, by fusing glass canes, or rods, in one or more colors to a core of yet another color.

The appearance of the glass bead may be altered further by the application of various surface treatments. The most common of these is an iridescent finish that gives the beads the rainbow sheen of oil floating on water. This permanent microcrystalline finish is achieved by applying a metallic chloride solution to the molten glass before it is stretched into a tube. The luster finish is similar, but with a whitish appearance. This finish on opaque beads imparts a pearlescent surface; these beads are sometimes referred to as Ceylon beads. Finally, salts of metals such as gold, bronze, or silver fired onto the surface of clear or black glass create beads that look as if they are made of those metals. It should be noted that some of these metallic finishes lack durability.

The appearance of transparent beads may be altered in yet another way by treatments to the hole in the bead itself. The interior of the hole may be lined with silver, gold, or paint that reflects through the glass of the bead. The hole may be square, creating internal facets that reflect light back through the bead. Additionally, the Japanese have found a way to etch the hole, creating yet another visual effect.

SIZING

Seed beads are graded in size from 5° to 22°. Size 5° is the largest, measuring about .120", and size 22° is the smallest, measuring about .040". Beads of the same type, but larger than size 5°, are not considered seed beads, but pony beads. Sizes under 16° are difficult to find, since the majority of these are no longer manufactured; thus, supplies are limited.

Seed beads may be either smooth-sided or faceted by cutting or molding. To make faceted beads, the worker threads ordinary seed beads onto a wire and passes the strand back and forth against a grinding wheel, cutting the beads' surface. Faceted beads come in various styles: three-cuts, having three facets cut into the side and one end; two-cuts, tiny cylinders with at least one cut or molded facet on the side; and one-cuts, or charlotte beads, which have a single hand-struck facet. Another type, the hex-cut, is not actually cut, but is extruded through a die that molds a glass tube with five or six sides. Last are bugle beads, which have the same diameters and finishes as the various seed beads, but are longer cylinders, ranging from one-eighth inch to two inches in length.

Appendix B
Basic Beadwork Techniques

Stringing beads on thread is the most elementary form of beadwork. The processes for producing beadwork of any complexity are based on such common fiber techniques as sewing, looping, and weaving. The exception is the attachment of individual beads with glue, paint, or wax. In creating beadwork, the artist either applies beads to a surface or unites them in a freestanding structure. Beadwork is either fabricated on a supporting framework, such as a loom, or worked off-loom, with needle and thread. Off-loom techniques allow the artist greater freedom to create an almost unlimited variety of structures and forms, while the loom aids in speed and uniformity. The beadwork techniques illustrated here are the primary methods employed by artists in creating the works presented in this book.

Open and Closed Daisy Chain

The daisy chain is a single-thread stitching technique. A small number of beads are strung and a circle is made by carrying the thread back through the first bead. A bead, generally of another color and sometimes larger, is then threaded on, and the needle is passed through one of the bottom beads in the circle, forming a daisy shape. To create an open daisy chain, a few beads are strung between each daisy. In a closed daisy chain, daisies are repeated contiguously. This simple technique is used most often to make necklaces or chains for medallions. The daisy chain is found in the work of Native Americans and some African groups, as well as in American and European jewelry from the 1960s and 1970s.

Peyote Stitch

The peyote stitch, sometimes called the gourd or twill stitch, is a single-thread technique that is worked back and forth for rectangular shapes and in a spiral or in rounds for circular shapes. Both the one-drop and two-drop variations begin with a thread of

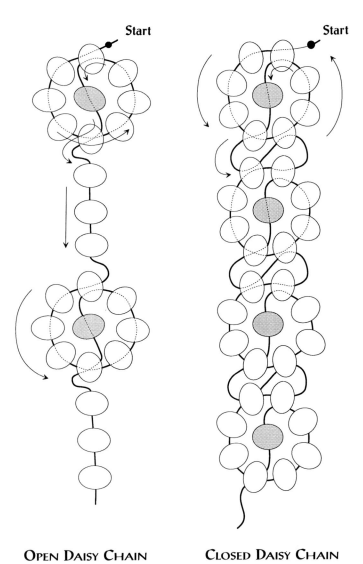

OPEN DAISY CHAIN　　　　**CLOSED DAISY CHAIN**

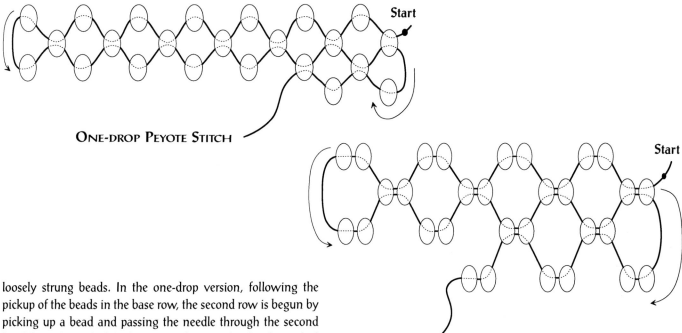

ONE-DROP PEYOTE STITCH

TWO-DROP PEYOTE STITCH

loosely strung beads. In the one-drop version, following the pickup of the beads in the base row, the second row is begun by picking up a bead and passing the needle through the second bead from the end of the base row; then another bead is picked up and the needle passes through the fourth bead from the end of the base row. Each time a bead is picked up, the needle is then passed through alternating beads in the row above. To form the two-drop peyote stitch, two beads are picked up instead of one, and the needle is passed through the third and fourth beads from the end of the base row. From then on, the needle picks up two beads and passes through two base-row beads. For circles, beads are added one at a time to form a circle. Then two beads are added and linked to a bead in the circle; then two more beads are added and linked once again, and so on, to complete another circle. On the next round, a single bead is added and linked between two beads in the previous circle. This pattern of rings is repeated, forming a flat disk.

The peyote stitch results in a flexible fabric, with the beads arranged in a twill pattern. This versatile technique permits the creation of almost any flat or sculptural structure, including rectangles, circles, tubes, spheres, and free-form shapes. This stitch may be self-supporting. It also may be worked over an armature or another object, such as a bottle, a branch, or a stone. The peyote stitch has its origins in the ancient cultures of the Middle East. In the new world Native Americans developed, and continue to use, a complex and unique form of this stitch. Many variations of the technique are used worldwide.

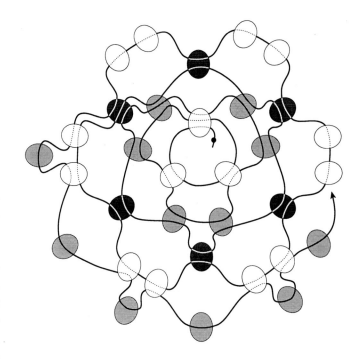

FLAT, CIRCULAR PEYOTE STITCH

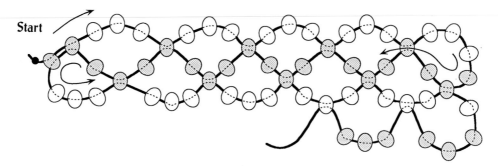

SINGLE-THREAD NETTING

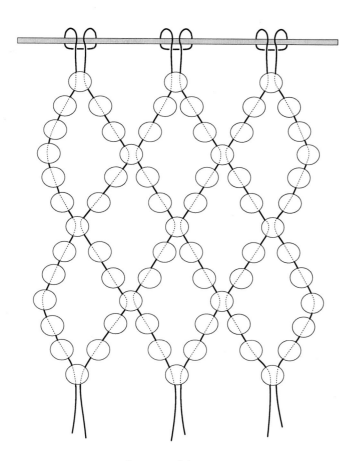

LATTICE NETTING

Netting

The netting technique, sometimes referred to as latticework or lattice stitch, results in a flexible, open mesh. There are two methods for creating this structure. The first, employing a single thread, is related to the peyote stitch in that it is worked back and forth, from side to side. It differs in that there are at least three beads, rather than one, between each anchor bead. The second method results in a mesh that appears almost identical to the first, but is formed by attaching multiple threads to a support, such as a string of beads, or the edge of some material, such as leather. This variation is worked from top to bottom, with the threads passed back and forth between the anchor beads. Adding extra threads at different points allows the shape to fan out, if flat, or to form a cone, if cylindrical. In both versions of the netting technique, the number of beads strung between each anchor bead affects not only the size of the mesh opening, but also the overall shape of the piece. Although this technique is well known and widespread, the Indonesians excel in its use.

Start

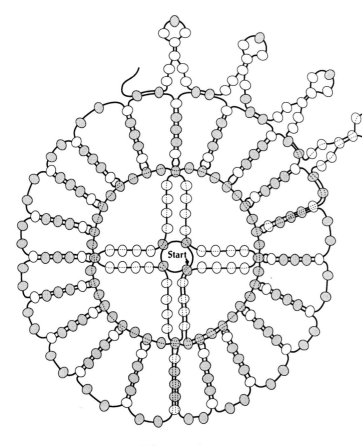

MANDALA

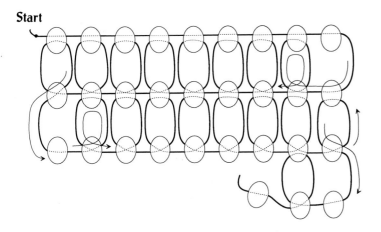

SQUARE STITCH

Mandala

A mandala is a variant of netting and looping techniques. The beginning is a circle of a few beads. Spokes of additional beads are attached to the beginning ring of beads and the work progresses outward in rounds, forming a lacy circle. A single mandala may be appliquéd to an object such as a garment or basket. It also may be connected to a daisy-chain necklace as a pendant, or several mandalas may be joined together to create a larger fabric. The mandala is a symbol of the universe — sometimes of the sun — and has religious significance in many cultures, particularly Hinduism and Buddhism.

Square Stitch

The square stitch technique begins with a simple string of beads. The second row is made by picking up two more beads and passing the thread up through the next-to-the-last bead on the needle-end of the base row. Then, the thread is pulled down between the two beads just added, and passed through the second of these beads, forming a square of four beads. To continue, a third bead is picked up and the thread is passed through the third bead from the end of the base row and circled back through the bead just added, and so on until the row is completed. Flat or dimensional structures are made by adding or omitting beads at certain points, as the work progresses. In this technique the beads are lined up side by side, directly above and below each other, and with thread showing between the rows; to the untrained eye, this has the appearance of loomed work. For this reason, the square stitch is sometimes referred to as the false loom-weave. The resulting fabric is somewhat rigid, due to the amount of thread passed through the beads.

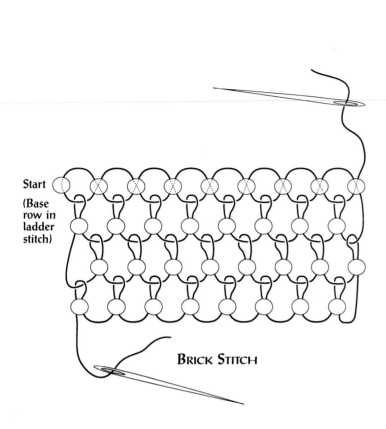

BRICK STITCH

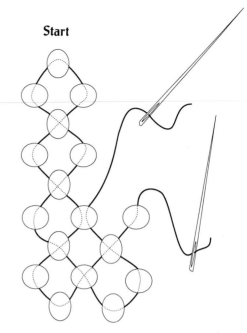

DOUBLE-NEEDLE RIGHT-ANGLE WEAVE

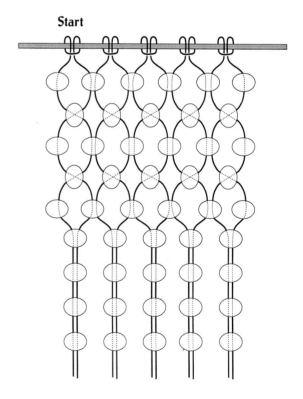

MULTIPLE-THREAD RIGHT-ANGLE WEAVE

Brick Stitch

The brick stitch is a looping technique in which two needles on one thread are used to form the base row of ladder stitch. Following the creation of the base row, only one of the two needles passes through the last bead, and picks up a bead. The threaded needle is then looped around the thread of the previous row and returned through the same bead. The work progresses one bead at a time. The pattern may be worked in almost any direction, which permits great flexibility in form and shape. The brick stitch is sometimes called Comanche stitch. This is an ancient technique used in cultures around the world, but especially in those of the Americas, the Middle East, and North Africa.

Right-angle Weave

The right-angle weave generally requires one thread and two needles. To begin, one of the needles picks up three beads which are slid to the center of the thread. A fourth bead is picked up on one needle, and the other needle is passed through this bead (an anchor bead) from the opposite direction so that the threads cross in the center of the bead. To continue, one more bead is picked up on each needle, then both threads cross in an additional bead. This technique results in a fabric in which one row of beads lies horizontally and the next lies vertically, in an alternating pattern. This technique may also be used with multiple threads in an even number. In this version, another design element may be added by stringing rows of beads on these extra strands between the sections of right-angle weave. Because of the complex nature of this technique, design considerations need to be thought out carefully. The fabric created has a flexible structure. Right-angle weave is used by the Mali of Africa and the indigenous peoples of the islands of New Guinea, Borneo, and the Philippines, and was popular in the late 1960s in Europe for jewelry and accessories.

Loom Weaving

The technique of loom weaving requires a framework that supports a quantity of warp threads with uniform tension. This framework may be a commercially produced or handmade bead loom, or even a bowed stick. Commercial bead looms usually have rollers at each end to accommodate long warps. These looms are not large and are suitable mostly for weaving narrow strips. However, a loom may be handmade for the specific size and shape of a given project. The weaving is begun by knotting a weft thread to an outside warp thread. Enough beads are placed on the weft for one bead to fill each space between the warp threads (one less than the number of warp threads). The weft thread, carrying the beads, is passed under the warp and the beads are pushed up between the warp threads. The needle with the weft thread is then passed back through the beads, over the top of the warp threads, securing them to the warp. This technique is frequently associated with Native Americans, but was also practiced extensively in Europe before World War I.

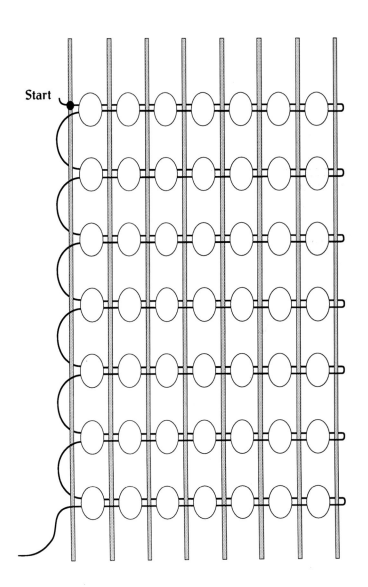

LOOM WEAVING

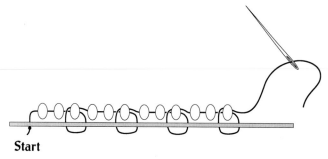

BACKSTITCH

Backstitch and Couching

The backstitch is an embroidery technique. From one to three beads at a time are picked up on a needle and sewn to a fabric or leather backing; then the thread is sewn back through one or more of these beads, before the next few beads are picked up and the process is repeated. The backstitch, an ancient technique, is in widespread use. In the couching stitch, beads are strung on one thread, which is sewn down with a second. Although this technique resembles the backstitch, it does not allow the artist the same fine control over the design.

Tambour Stitch

The tambour stitch, another embroidery stitch, requires a special needle, which resembles a tiny crochet hook. Fabric is stretched on a hoop, or tambour, with the underside facing up, and the work below. The string of beads forming the design is secured temporarily to the side facing down. The tambour hook is pushed down through the material and picks up a loop of thread between two beads. This loop is pulled through to the back and remains around the hook, which is then pushed down through the material again and picks up another loop between beads farther down the strand. The second loop is pulled through the first, fastening the beads to the front surface. When the hooking is completed, the back of the fabric is covered with chains of interlocked loops, while the front is covered with the beaded design. Without examining the back of the material, it would be impossible to determine that the beads had not been sewn in place by another technique. The tambour technique is used for both linear contour beading and fields of beads, and is found in India, North Africa, and Asia. In Europe and North America it has been used mostly by the fashion industry to embellish clothing and accessories, since beads may be applied more rapidly this way than by sewing.

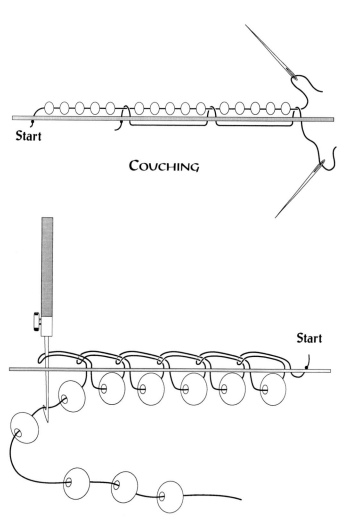

COUCHING

TAMBOUR STITCH

Glossary

Anchor bead. A bead inside which two or more threads cross, locking its position and preventing the movement of the beads to either side of it. Also, a bead through which two or more threads pass in the same direction, securing the bead.

Armature. A durable, three-dimensional framework or skeleton that provides the interior support of a sculpture.

Assemblage. A form of sculpture created by arranging combinations of assorted found objects, parts, and materials, sometimes incorporating painting, drawing, or photography.

Backstitch. An embroidery stitch used to sew a line of seed beads to a backing, usually of leather, canvas, or other cloth. From one to three beads are attached with a simple stitch, then the thread is sewn back through one or more of these beads, and the stitch is repeated.

Bead loom. A device that supports a warp of threads for handweaving a beaded fabric. Commercially produced bead looms are constructed of metal, wood, or rigid plastic, with rollers at each end to accommodate fabric as it is woven.

Beadwork. Art created with small, uniform beads (generally seed beads), in which the beads are subordinate to the overall form and design of the entire piece. Beadwork may be considered a form of fiber art, since the beads are usually supported on a filament, such as thread or wire, which is handled like any other fiber; the exception is when beads are affixed with an adhesive, such as glue or wax.

Blowpipe. A long metal tube, usually of iron or steel, through which a glassworker blows air into a gather, or blob of molten glass, collected on the end of the tube.

Brain tanning. A primitive method for curing leather in which fresh animal brains are rubbed into raw hide. The brains contain enzymes that cause chemical reactions that preserve the hide.

Brick stitch. A beadwork technique in which thread is passed through one bead, looped around the thread of the row directly above that bead, and returned through the same bead. Another bead is then picked up and the process is repeated. This technique is sometimes referred to as Comanche stitch because of its extensive use by that Native American tribe.

Broadcollar. A circular neckpiece with a central neck opening, whose sides extend from shoulder to shoulder when worn. A style of jewelry favored by the ancient Egyptians.

Bugle bead. A tiny, tubular glass bead. Bugle beads vary in length from one-eighth inch to two inches and have the same variety of finishes and diameters as do standard seed beads.

Cathedral glass. A type of glass that is completely transparent, with saturated color and high light refraction.

Ceylon bead. An opaque glass seed bead with a permanent pearlized finish.

Charlotte bead. A seed bead with a single hand-cut facet.

Comanche stitch. *See* Brick stitch.

Contour beading. An embroidery technique in which rows of beads are stitched around a central shape, following and amplifying the contours of the shape.

Copal amber. A soft natural resin that is formed into beads, using heat and pressure; the finished product resembles real amber, which is fossilized tree sap. These beads are common in many parts of Africa and became popular in the United States and Europe in the 1960s.

Couching. An embroidery technique used to attach beads strung on one thread to a backing by stitching a second thread over the first between groups of beads.

Crocheted beadwork. A needlework technique in which bead-strung thread is interwoven in loops, by means of a single hooked needle. The crochet hook does not pass through the beads, but is used to hook only the thread, which locks the beads in place between the loops.

Cut bead. A glass seed bead that has hand-cut or molded facets. Two-cut beads have faceted sides. Three-cuts have faceted sides and ends.

Daisy chain. A beadwork stitch in which bead circles resembling flowers are fashioned by stringing a circle of beads on a thread, which is then passed through the center, picking up another bead, and out through the bead opposite the starting point. A chain of "daisies" is fashioned by repeating the stitch, sometimes with additional beads between flowers.

Drawn glass. Semimolten glass that is stretched by hand or machine to produce elongated tubes or sheets of uniform thickness.

Drawn-glass bead. A bead made from a lateral slice of a drawn-glass tube. This process permits the mass production of large quantities of uniform beads in a wide variety of sizes, colors, and finishes.

False loom-weave. *See* Square stitch.

Fire-polished bead. A glass bead with a smooth, shiny finish, achieved when it is reheated just enough to melt the surface.

Floating warp. An area of warp where the threads are left free and unwoven. In beadwork these warp threads may be strung with beads before they are attached to the loom, so that the beadworker can design sections of strung beads bounded by sections of woven beads.

Gather. In glassworking, the ball of molten glass collected on the end of a long metal tube or blowpipe.

Gemstone bead. A bead made from any semiprecious stone or mineral, such as agate or garnet. Amber, coral, jet, pearls, and ivory may be included in this category.

Greasy glass. A semiopaque glass with a soft, oily sheen.

Hank. Several strands of beads looped and tied in a bunch for ease in marketing. The number of beads in a hank is determined by weight, with the number and length of strands depending on the size and type of bead.

Heishi. A small, uniform, disk-shaped bead. *Heishi* are made in many parts of the world from such materials as turquoise, seashell, ostrich eggshell, and coconut shell. Roughed-out, pierced disks are strung on a wire and rubbed on an abrasive surface such as stone until the disks are uniform in size and have smooth edges. The term comes from the Keresan language of the Pueblo Indian tribes of New Mexico.

Hex-cut bead. A faceted seed bead with five or six sides that is not cut, but made from molded glass.

Iris or iridescent bead. A glass bead with a coating that creates a rainbow effect.

Ladder stitch. A beadwork technique in which a chain or ladder of beads is formed using two threaded needles, which enter each bead from opposite sides, crossing inside it.

Lattice stitch, or latticework. *See* Netting.

Lazy stitch. A beadwork technique in which large areas of pattern are filled in by stitching three or more beads at a time in parallel rows. A decorative technique developed by Native Americans that derived from, and eventually replaced, the use of porcupine quills.

Lined bead. A transparent bead whose appearance or color has been altered by treatments to its hole. The interior of the hole may be lined with silver or gold foil, which is applied before the glass tube is drawn. After a bead is manufactured its appearance may be altered by forcing paint into the hole, where it reflects through the glass. Additionally, the hole may be etched, creating yet another visual effect.

Luster bead. A glass bead with a semitransparent coating that has a high gloss with a whitish appearance.

Macrame. A technique for creating textiles through elaborate knotting of fibers, onto which beads may be strung.

Mandala. A traditional circular composition containing concentric geometric designs, images, or patterns. In many beliefs, especially Hinduism and Buddhism, this circular form represents the sun or the totality of the universe and may serve as a focus for meditation.

Matte bead. A glass bead with a dull, low-luster surface produced by etching in an acid bath or by tumbling.

Metallic oxides and salts. Metallic compounds composed of molecules containing the elements oxygen or chlorine. One or more of these compounds in powdered form is added to clear molten glass to impart color as well as other characteristics, such as elasticity and opacity. For example, brown glass results from the addition of ferric oxide, commonly known as rust.

Microbead. A bead with a diameter of between .040" and .240". Glass and metal seed beads fall into this category.

Molded bead. A textured bead made when a semimolten glass tube is pressed into a mold, usually consisting of two parts, by hand or machine.

Netting. A beadwork technique, sometimes referred to as lattice stitch, or latticework, that results in a flexible, open mesh of beads. There are two methods for creating this structure: the first employs a single thread that is worked back and forth, from side to side, passing through a shared (anchor) bead every few beads; the second employs multiple threads tied at regular intervals to a support and worked from top to bottom.

Off-loom technique. Any fiber or beadwork technique that does not require the use of a loom or supporting frame for the thread.

One-drop and two-drop peyote stitch. Two of the many variations on the peyote-stitch technique. One-drop peyote stitch involves alternating the twill pattern every other bead; in two-drop stitch it is alternated every two beads.

Opalescent glass. A glass with a translucent, slightly clouded, yet colorful appearance, produced by the addition of chemical compounds while it is molten.

Pectoral. A type of neckpiece in which components extend from a necklace down the front of the wearer, lying against the chest.

Peyote stitch. A beadwork technique with many variants, sometimes referred to as gourd or twill stitch, that results in a flexible, yet solid, textile in which the beads form a twill pattern. It is a single-needle technique that is worked back and forth for rectangular shapes, and in a spiral or in rounds for circular or tubular shapes. The name derives from traditional Native American implements, covered with this style of beadwork, used in the Southwest in a religious ceremony involving the peyote cactus; the technique, however, is ancient.

Pony bead. A glass bead that is shaped and used like a seed bead, but is larger; the largest have a diameter of one-quarter inch. The name is said to derive either from the use of horses to transport them, or from their use in horse regalia.

Random-dot bleed pattern. A pattern in beadwork in which, in a field of beads of one color, the number of beads of a contrasting color is gradually increased over several rows to create the effect of one color fading or bleeding into another.

Reversing symmetry. A type of symmetry in which the colors, shapes, or patterns of the background and foreground reverse at the central axis of a composition, distorting the perspective and creating a sense of vibration.

Right-angle weave. A beadwork technique in which one row of beads lies horizontally and the next lies vertically, forming a tight mesh of open squares. One version of the right-angle weave uses two threaded needles and a single thread. Another uses an even number of threads, anchored at one end.

Satin glass. A translucent glass with a tone-on-tone appearance, created during manufacture: either by working air bubbles into the gather, or by fusing glass strands of the same color to the outside of the gather before it is drawn or shaped. The result is a glass with a striated look, resembling watered silk.

Seed bead. A glass or metal microbead. Seed beads are made in standard sizes and in a wide range of colors, textures, and finishes. They serve as a medium for creating a variety of art forms from sculpture to embroidery.

Seeding stitch. An embroidery technique in which each seed bead is attached with a single stitch in random order.

Spirit bead. A single bead of a different color or type incorporated into a piece of beadwork. The significance of this bead relates to the ancient tradition of Navajo weavers, who wove a subtle design known as the spirit path into each weaving to prevent the spirit of the weaver from becoming trapped in the work.

Split complements. In color theory, a triad of colors that includes a hue and the two hues located to either side of its complement on the color wheel. For example, the split complements of yellow are blue-violet and red-violet.

Square stitch. A beadwork technique that resembles loomed work and is sometimes referred to as false loom-weave. Starting with a string of beads, each new row is begun by picking up two more beads and passing the thread through the penultimate bead of the previous row and back through the second of the beads just added, to form a square of four beads. After that, the row is completed by adding one bead at a time, so that the beads are arranged side by side, directly above and below each other, with the thread showing between the rows.

Supplementary warp. Additional threads added at any point within or to the sides of the original warp to change the size and shape of a weaving.

Tambour stitch. An embroidery technique that requires a special needle resembling a tiny crochet hook. The work is done from the back on fabric stretched on a hoop, or tambour. A string of beads that will form the design is secured to the side of the cloth facing down, and the tambour hook is then pushed down through the fabric to pull up a loop of thread from between two beads. This is repeated, with each loop interlocking with the previous one, so that when the hooking is completed, the back of the fabric is covered by chains of interlocked loops, while the front is covered with the beaded design.

Trade bead. Any bead used in barter and trade around the world. The term most commonly refers to beads manufactured in Europe, beginning in the sixteenth century, and traded in Africa for slaves and raw materials.

Warp. The set of threads stretched lengthwise on a loom that form the vertical axis of a woven textile.

Weft. In beadweaving, the thread that carries the beads and is woven back and forth across the warp to create a beaded textile. More generally, the horizontal threads of a woven textile, not strung on the loom, but woven back and forth.

White-heart bead. A bead made with two layers of glass fused one over the other. The outer layer, a transparent colored glass, covers an opaque core, usually white.

Wound bead. A bead formed by winding molten glass around a wire or rod, which leaves a hole when removed.

Exhibitions

"Beads in Art and Fashion," June 14–June 30, 1980, A Gallery, Stinson Beach, California. Curated by Robin Cohen.

"Good as Gold: Alternative Materials in American Jewelry," traveling exhibition, December 1, 1981–March 28, 1982, Renwick Gallery, Smithsonian Institution, Washington, D.C. Curated by Lloyd E. Herman. Exh. cat.

"Bead It!" December 13, 1985–April 13, 1986, San Diego Museum of Man, California.

"Pictorial Beadwork," January 12–February 19, 1986, Southern Plains Indian Museum and Crafts Center, Anadarko, Oklahoma.

"The Bead Goes On: Expressions in Contemporary Beadwork," traveling exhibition, January 1987–December 1988, Visual Arts Resources, University of Oregon Museum of Art, Eugene. Curated by Candace Moffett and Alice Scherer.

"The Paul and Joyce Show," January 8–April 4, 1987, Maryland Art Place, Baltimore. Exh. cat.

"The Ubiquitous Bead," September 5–October 25, 1987, Bellevue Art Museum, Bellevue, Washington. Curated by Ramona Solberg.

"Beads," October 14–December 23, 1987, Tambaran Gallery, New York City. Curated by Lois Sherr Dubin.

"Structure and Surface: Beads in Contemporary American Art," December 4, 1988–February 12, 1989, John Michael Kohler Art Center, Sheboygan, Wisconsin; July 27–November 25, 1990, Renwick Gallery, Smithsonian Institution, Washington, D.C. Curated by Mark Richard Leach. Exh. cat.

"Contemporary Plains Indian Moccasins," January 15–February 15, 1989, Southern Plains Indian Museum and Crafts Center, Anadarko, Oklahoma.

"A Moment in Africa: One Man's Collection of Beadwork," February 2–May 13, 1989, Center for the Study of Beadwork, Portland, Oregon. Curated by Alice Scherer.

"Contemporary Beaded Bags," May 18–July 29, 1989, Center for the Study of Beadwork, Portland, Oregon. Curated by Alice Scherer.

"Selections from the Study Collection of the Center for the Study of Beadwork," August 3–October 28, 1989, Center for the Study of Beadwork, Portland, Oregon. Curated by Alice Scherer.

"Great Scott!!: The Beadwork of Joyce J. Scott," November 2, 1989–January 27, 1990, Center for the Study of Beadwork, Portland, Oregon. Curated by Alice Scherer.

"The Well-Dressed Horse: An Exhibition of Beaded Indian Horse Gear," February 1–April 28, 1990, Center for the Study of Beadwork, Portland, Oregon. Curated by Mariana Mace.

"Beadazzled: Costume Embellishment of the Early Twentieth Century," April 15–June 24, 1990, Hudson River Museum, Yonkers, New York. Curated by Laura L. V. Hardin.

"The Glass Bead Game," April 23–June 6, 1991, Illumina Gallery, Atlanta, Georgia. Curated by Pat Poole.

"Joyce Scott: I-con-no-body/I-con-no-graphy," September 13–November 15, 1991, Corcoran Gallery of Art, Washington D.C. Curated by Terri Sultan. Exh. cat.

"Beadazzled," December 7, 1991–January 4, 1992, Sybaris Gallery, Royal Oaks, Michigan.

Selected Bibliography

"Beaded Fish" (the beadwork of Christine Olsen Reis). *Threads*. 11 (June–July 1987): back cover.

Behn, Maya. *Verena Sieber-Fuchs*. Exh. cat. Zurich: Maya Behn Galerie, 1984.

Benesh, Carolyn L. E. "Message through the Veil: Joyce Scott's Beaded Jewelry." *Ornament* 10 (Winter 1986): 32–33, 78.

———. "Newcomb Company: Fine Porcelain Jewelry." *Ornament* 10 (Winter 1986): 26–31.

Blakelock, Virginia. "How to Play the Glass-Bead Game." *Threads* 20 (December 1988–January 1989): 66–71.

Buraimoh, Jimoh. "Painting with Beads." *African Arts* 5 (Autumn 1971): 16–19.

———. *Turning Point: An Exhibition of Bead Works and Paintings*. Exh. cat. Lagos, Nigeria: National Museum, 1991.

Clabburn, Pamela. *Beadwork*. Aylesbury, Eng.: Shire Publications, 1980.

Constantine, Mildred, and Jack Lenor Larsen. *Beyond Craft: The Art Fabric*. New York: Van Nostrand, Reinhold, 1972.

———. *The Art Fabric: Mainstream*. New York: Van Nostrand, Reinhold, 1981.

Courtney-Clarke, Margaret. *Ndebele*. New York: Rizzoli, 1986.

Dale, Julie Schafler. *Art to Wear*. New York: Abbeville, 1986.

Davis, Ray C. *Prize Winners: Twelve Loomed Necklaces*. Phoenix, Ariz.: Creative Bead Supplies, 1977.

DeLange, Deon. *Techniques of Beading Earrings*. Ogden, Utah: Eagle's View Publishing, 1983.

———. *More Techniques of Beading Earrings*. Ogden, Utah: Eagle's View Publishing, 1985.

Dubin, Lois Sherr. *The History of Beads*. New York: Harry N. Abrams, 1987.

Edwards, Joan. *Berlin Work*. Dorking, Eng.: Bayford Books, 1980.

———. *Bead Embroidery*. London: B. T. Batsford, 1966.

———. "Tambour Beading." *Costume* 3 (1969): 61–64.

Erikson, Joan Mowat. *The Universal Bead*. New York: W. W. Norton, 1969.

Erlandsen, Ida-Merete, and Hetty Mooi. *The Bead Book: Sewing and Weaving with Beads*. New York: Van Nostrand, Reinhold, 1974.

Fagg, William. *Yoruba Beadwork: Art of Nigeria*. New York: Rizzoli, 1980.

Farlie, Barbara L. *Beading: Basic and Boutique*. Des Moines, Iowa: Creative Home Library, 1971.

Fiberarts Design Book, 4 vols. Asheville, N.C.: Lark Books, 1980, 1983, 1987, 1991.

Fisher, Angela. *Africa Adorned*. New York: Harry N. Abrams, 1984.

"Follow-up (More on Mary B. Hetz)." *Ornament* 8 (1985): 31.

Francis, Peter, Jr. "Bead Report XVIII: The Asian Bead Study Tour IV, A Little Tube of Glass." *Ornament* 10 (Autumn 1986): 54–57, 74–76.

———. *The Czech Bead Story*. Lake Placid, N.Y.: Lapis Route Books, 1979.

———. *A Handbook of Bead Materials*. Lake Placid, N.Y.: Lapis Route Books, 1982.

———. *A Short Dictionary of Bead Terms and Types*. Lake Placid, N.Y.: Lapis Route Books, 1979. Rev. and enl., 1989.

Glassman, Judith. *Step by Step Beadcraft*. New York: Golden Press, 1974.

Goldberg, JoAnn. "Julie Schafler Dale: Art-to-Wear Visionary." *Ornament* 10 (Winter 1986): 42–47.

Goodhue, Horace. *Indian Bead-Weaving Patterns*. Saint Paul, Minn.: Bead-Craft, 1975. 3d rev. ed., 1989.

Harris, Elizabeth. *A Bead Primer*. Prescott, Ariz.: Bead Museum, 1987.

Herman, Lloyd E. *Good as Gold*. Exh. cat. Washington, D.C.: Smithsonian Institution, 1981.

Hunt, W. Ben, and J. F. "Buck" Burshears. *American Indian Beadwork*. Milwaukee: Bruce Publishing, 1951.

Jacopetti, Alexandra. *Native Funk and Flash*. San Francisco: Scrimshaw Press, 1974.

Kennedy, S. S. J. "Juxtaposition: Beaded Belts." *Ornament* 7 (1983): 58.

"Marketplace: Mary B. Hetz." *Ornament* 7 (1983): 38–39.

Kidd, Kenneth E., and Martha Ann Kidd. *A Classification System for Glass Beads for the Use of Field Archaeologists*. Ottawa: National Historic Sites Service, 1970.

Kliot, Jules, and Kaethe Kliot, eds. *Bead Work*. Berkeley: Lacis Publications, 1984.

LaCroix, Grethe. *Creating with Beads*. New York: Sterling Publishing, 1969.

Laessig, Joanne Alford. "Getting Started in Bead Embroidery." *Flying Needle* 18 (August 1989): 16–19.

Leach, Mark Richard. *Structure and Surface: Beads in Contemporary American Art*. Exh. cat. Sheboygan, Wisc.: John Michael Kohler Arts Center, 1990.

Lillie, Jacqueline. *Perlenschmuck* [Beads at Work]. Vienna, Austria: J. I. Lillie, 1991.

Orchard, William C. *Beads and Beadwork of the American Indians*. New York: Museum of the American Indian, Heye Foundation, 1929. Reprint, 1975.

The Paul and Joyce Show. Exh. cat. Baltimore: Maryland Art Place, 1987.

Poris, Ruth F. *Advanced Beadwork*. Tampa, Fla.: Golden Hands Press, 1989.

Sleen, Wicher Gosen Nicholaas van der. *A Handbook on Beads*. York, Pa.: George Shumway, 1967.

Spears, Therese. *Beaded Clothing Techniques*. Boulder, Colo.: Promenade, 1984.

———. *Beaded Earrings*. Boulder, Colo.: Promenade, 1984.

———. *Contemporary Loomed Beadwork*. Boulder, Colo.: Promenade, 1987.

Thompson, Angela. *Embroidery with Beads*. London: B. T. Batsford, 1987.

Tomalin, Stefany. *Beads! Make Your Own Unique Jewellery*. Newton Abbot, Eng.: David and Charles Publishers, 1988.

Weber, Betty J., and Anne Duncan. *Simply Beads*. Culver City, Calif.: Western Trimming Corporation, 1971.

White, Mary. *How to Do Beadwork*. New York: Dover, 1972.

Woodsmall, Annabel Whitney. *Contemporary Appliqued Beadwork*. Freeland, Wash.: HTH Publications, 1979.

Young, Jean. *Woodstock Craftsman Manual*. New York: Praeger, 1972.

Associations and Resources

Bead Societies

Most of these groups hold meetings with invited speakers once a month, usually on a designated day, frequently with no meeting scheduled for August or December. Most have monthly newsletters.

ARIZONA BEAD SOCIETY
Box 80111, Arcadia Station 072
Phoenix, Arizona 85060-0111

AUSTIN BEAD SOCIETY
P.O. Box 656
Austin, Texas 78767-0656

BALTIMORE BEAD SOCIETY
P.O. Box 311
Riderwood, Maryland 21139-0311

BEADESIGNER INTERNATIONAL
P.O. Box 503
Lincoln, Massachusetts 01773

BEAD SOCIETY OF CENTRAL FLORIDA
121 Larkspur Drive
Altamonte Springs, Florida 32701

BEAD SOCIETY OF CENTRAL OHIO, C/O BYZANTIUM
245 King Avenue
Columbus, Ohio 43201

BEAD SOCIETY OF GREAT BRITAIN, C/O CAROLE MORRIS
1 Casburn Lane
Burwell, Cambridgeshire CB5 0ED
England

BEAD SOCIETY OF GREATER CHICAGO
8420 W. Bryn Mawr Avenue, #600
Chicago, Illinois 60631

BEAD SOCIETY OF GREATER NEW YORK, C/O FASHION INSTITUTE OF TECHNOLOGY
227 W. 27th Street, Room A605
New York, New York 10001

BEAD SOCIETY OF GREATER WASHINGTON
P.O. Box 70036
Chevy Chase, Maryland 20813-0036

BEAD SOCIETY OF LOS ANGELES
P.O. Box 241874
Los Angeles, California 90024-9674

BEAD SOCIETY OF NEW JERSEY
P.O. Box 7465
Shrewsbury, New Jersey 07702

CHICAGO MIDWEST BEAD SOCIETY
1020 Davis Street
Evanston, Illinois 60201

GREAT LAKES BEADWORKERS GUILD
P.O. Box 1639
Royal Oak, Michigan 48068

JUNEAU BEAD SOCIETY, C/O THE BEAD GALLERY
201 Seward
Juneau, Alaska 99801

NEW MEXICO BEAD SOCIETY
P.O. Box 36824
Albuquerque, New Mexico 87176

NORTHERN CALIFORNIA BEAD SOCIETY
1650 Lower Grand Avenue
Piedmont, California 94611

NORTHWEST BEAD SOCIETY
3213 W. Wheeler Street, ste. 517
Seattle, Washington 98199

OLYMPIC BEAD SOCIETY
P.O. Box 27
Quilcene, Washington 98376

PORTLAND BEAD SOCIETY
P.O. Box 10611
Portland, Oregon 97210

ROCKY MOUNTAIN BEAD SOCIETY
1633 F Fourth Street
Boulder, Colorado 80302

UPPER MIDWEST BEAD SOCIETY, C/O BEAUTIFUL BEADS
115 Hennepin Avenue
Minneapolis, Minnesota 55401

Research Foundations

The following organizations are devoted to the study of beads. Each offers memberships, with regular newsletters.

BEAD MUSEUM C/O GABRIELLE LIESE
140 S. Montezuma
Prescott, Arizona 86301

BEAD STUDY TRUST C/O FLORA WESTLAKE
Talland
Fullers Road
Rowledge, Farnham, Surrey GU10 4DF
England

CENTER FOR BEAD RESEARCH C/O PETER FRANCIS, JR.
4 Essex Street
Lake Placid, New York 12946

CENTER FOR THE STUDY OF BEADWORK C/O ALICE SCHERER
P.O. Box 13719
Portland, Oregon 97213

SOCIETY FOR BEAD RESEARCHERS C/O LESTER ROSS
Secretary-Treasurer
56489 El Dorado Drive
Yucca Valley, California 92284-4230

Sources of Beadwork Supplies

ART TO WEAR
4202 Water Oaks Lane
Tampa, Florida 33624
(813) 265-1681
Contact: Bob Poris

BEADER'S PARADISE
P.O. Box 362
Blackfoot, Idaho 83221
(208) 785-9967 or 785-1838
Contact: Wilma Mangum

BEADS BEADS
949 N. Tustin Avenue
Orange, California 92667
(714) 639-1611
Contact: Chuck Paddock and Lorena Holman

BEAD SHOP OF PALO ALTO (99 BEADS)
177 Hamilton Avenue
Palo Alto, California 94301
(800) 992-3237
Contact: Winnie Gooch

BEAD SHOPPE c/o GICK PUBLISHING
9 Studebaker
Irvine, California 92718
(714) 581-5830
Contact: James Gick

BEADWORKS
126 W. Third Avenue
Vancouver, British Columbia V5Y 1E9
Canada
(604) 876-6637
Contact: Graeme Teixeira

BEADWORKS INTERNATIONAL
139 Washington Street
Norwalk, Connecticut 06854
(203) 852-9194
Contact: Nancy Wall and Stephen Sammons

BERGER SPECIALTY COMPANY
413 E. Eighth Street
Los Angeles, California 90014
(213) 627-8783

BOVIS BEAD COMPANY
220 E. Fremont Street
P.O. Box 460
Tombstone, Arizona 85638
(602) 457-3359
Contact: Pierre or Shirley Bovis

CRAZY CROW TRADING POST
107 N. Fannin
Denison, Texas 75020
(214) 463-1366; Contact: Rex Reddick

EAGLECRAFTS
168 W. 12th Street
Ogden, Utah 84404-5501
(801) 393-3991; Contact: Monte Smith

ELLIOT, GREENE AND COMPANY
37 W. 37th Street
New York, New York 10018
(212) 391-9075; Contact: Allan Shore, Jr.

GARDEN OF BEADIN'
P.O. Box 1535
Redway, California 95560
(707) 943-3829
Contact: Charlotte Silverstein

GENERAL BEAD
637 Minna Street
San Francisco, California 94103
(415) 621-8187
Contact: Steven Sunshine

GYPSY WIND BEADS AND TRIM
147 Sacramento Street
Auburn, California 95603
(916) 823-1020; Contact: Judee Webb

HAR-MAN IMPORTING
16 W. 37th Street
New York, New York 10018
(212) 947-1440; Contact: Jack Mandel

HELBY IMPORT COMPANY
74 Rupert Avenue
Staten Island, New York 10314
(718) 447-0008
Contact: Larry Weiss
For the trade only

INTERNATIONAL BEAD AND SEQUIN
P.O. Box 585445
Dallas, Texas 75258
(214) 216-1592
Contact: Tammi Green

ORB WEAVER
4793 Telegraph Avenue
Oakland, California 94609
Contact: Jean Astrinsky

ORNAMENTAL RESOURCES
P.O. Box 3010
Idaho Springs, Colorado 80452
(303) 279-2102; Contact: Irma Fleming

PROMENADE ENTERPRISES
P.O. Box 2092
Boulder, Colorado 80306
(303) 440-4807; Contact: Therese Spears

RINGS AND THINGS
814 W. Main Avenue
P.O. Box 450 (mail)
Spokane, Washington 99210
(509) 624-8565; Contact: Russ Nobbs

RIO GRANDE JEWELERS SUPPLY
6901 Washington N.E.
Albuquerque, New Mexico 87109
(505) 345-8511

SHIPWRECK BEADS
5021 Mud Bay Road
Olympia, Washington 98502
(206) 866-4061
Contact: Glenn and Lisa Vincent

WESTERN TRADING POST
P.O. Box 9070 CSB
32 Broadway
Denver, Colorado 80209-0070
(303) 777-7750; Contact: Ron Eberhart

For information about additional sources of bead supplies, contact The Bead Directory, P.O. Box 10103, Oakland, CA 94610.

An additional source of information and the only publication consistently to cover bead-related topics is:

ORNAMENT
P.O. Box 2349
San Marcos, California 92079
(800) 888-8950

Acknowledgments

THE NEW BEADWORK could not have become a book without the assistance, support, and generosity of a great many people. First and foremost, we are indebted to Lois Sherr Dubin for her faith in the project and her unwavering commitment to it. Thanks go to Margaret Kaplan, senior vice-president and executive editor of Harry N. Abrams, Inc., for shepherding it from idea to printed book.

We are grateful to John Lottes, formerly of the Oregon School of Arts and Crafts in Portland, and his board of trustees, for agreeing to act as our umbrella organization. Sara Whiteley kindly made the initial suggestion and Marcella McGee graciously added administration of the grant monies to her other responsibilities.

Thanks to Tommy Olof Elder for his superb photographs, and to Andrea Leskes, his wife, and Ambjorn Elder, their son, for their hospitality while the artworks were being photographed. We appreciated the loan of a mannequin from the F. B. Fogg company of Muncie, Indiana, and the assistance of Millie Edwards of the Boston YWCA during the last photography session.

The photography was made possible by the generosity of several grantors: Jean Vollum, Stan Gillis, Katharine M. Honea, Mary Dickey, and Ann Ziff. Other grant assistance came from Jean Coughlin, Joanne Van Ness, John M. Evey, Valerie Hector, and Cecile Bass.

The following proprietors of bead stores and trading posts offered much assistance: Irma Fleming, Allan Shore, Jr., Glenn and Lisa Vincent, Chuck Paddock, Judee Webb, Nancy Wall, Pierre Bovis, Chuck Wulfmueller, James Gick, Therese Spears, Russ Nobbs, Jack Mandel, Larry Weiss, and Winnie Gooch; Graeme Teixeira; Vladimir Vesely, Jablonex Foreign Trade Company, Ltd., the representative for the Czechoslovakian bead industry in the United States; and the Ceske Perlicky Company of Zasada, Czechoslovakia.

Among bead societies and their members, our particular thanks go to Nicolette Stessin, Northwest Bead Society; Gabrielle Liese, Arizona Bead Society; Dorothy Walker, New Mexico Bead Society; and especially the Los Angeles Bead Society, which provided funds for a valuable slide bank.

We appreciate the artists' representatives who acted as vitally important liaisons: Roland Crawford, Lawrence Tafoya, Rosanne Raab Associates, Shawn Ferris, Mario Klimiades, Cindi Bogart, Suzanne Scarcella, Artwear, and Obiko. Initial contact with many of the artists was provided by the staff of Visual Arts Resources at the University of Oregon, Eugene. Particular thanks go to Michael Whitenack, Becky Slade, Stephen Deck, and Candace Moffett.

For general support and technical services, we offer special thanks to Michael and Nikki Fay, the staff of Hise Photography Studio, Dennis Venable, Alan Bates, Mike Hoffman, Nicola Porreco, Ernest Reyes, Becky Kuehne, Jackie Farris, Sue Foran, Christina Washington O'Bryan, Anne Smith, Ron Huhn, Cara King, Ramona Solberg, Joyce Scott, Chris Carmer, Joyce Cherry, Hank Scherer, Juhree and Don Noviello, and Janice Kersey Marshall. Thanks also to Peter Francis, Jr., Hallie Katz, and Wilma Mangum for needed research materials. Additional encouragement and support came from our fellow beadwork writers Horace Goodhue, Margret Carey, Susanne Aikman, Stefany Tomalin, Therese Spears, Evelyn Ulzen, and the late Ruth Poris.

Our most special gratitude goes to Howard Newcomb and Dennis Moss, to Elizabeth Newcomb and Adriane Moss, for message taking, mailing, editing and typing, suggestions, and general aid and comfort.

And finally, a very special thank-you to all the artists who appear in this book and several who do not, who cheered us on, tracked down pieces for us to photograph, shared resources, and answered our call for "dream pieces" by creating works especially for the book. Our thanks to those who understood what we set out to do and responded with appreciation and encouragement.

Photograph and Illustration Credits

Numbers refer to pages.

Photography, other than by Tommy Olof Elder: Gary Betts, 27; Eduardo Calderon, courtesy Linda Farris Gallery, Seattle, Washington, 62; Eric Griswold, 64 bottom; Dennis Hellawell, 54, 55; Dan King-Lehman, 53 top; Michael Lichter, 43 left; Paul Macapia, 61; Alan Magayne-Roshak, 50; Alice Scherer, 26, 71; Georg Stark, 83; Kanji Takeno, 81 top, 82; Urschel Laboratories, Inc., 89; E. K. Waller, 52, 53 top; C. Wolters, 91 bottom; Wong Wang Fai, 37 left.

Illustrations, 96–102, are by Howard Newcomb. Models are Heather K. Angell, 27; Lashawnnya Thomas, 81; and Mariana Zantrop, 28.

Index